ORGANIZING FOR MINISTRY AND MISSION

Options for Church Structure

David J. Peter

CONCORDIA PUBLISHING HOUSE • SAINT LOUIS

This book is dedicated to my parents,
Victor and Arliss Peter,
who taught me to love Christ and
His Church, and who inspired me
to serve God and His people.

Published by Concordia Publishing House
3558 S. Jefferson Avenue, St. Louis, MO 63118-3968
1-800-325-3040 • cph.org

Manufactured in the United States of America

Library of Congress Cataloging-in-Publication Data

Names: Peter, David J., author.

Title: Organizing for ministry and mission : options for church structure congregations / David J. Peter.

Description: Saint Louis, MO : Concordia Publishing House, [2023] | Summary: "This book is a resource to advance fruitful mission and ministry by improving the organizational design and administrative practices of congregations. Dr. Peter identifies the theological and practical reasons for organizing staff, lay officers, and congregational volunteers. He presents three dominant models for organizing churches and identifies the advantages and disadvantages of each. This book guides church officers to maximize the effectiveness of their congregations' organizational design. It equips board leaders for fruitful service to the Lord and His people. Pastors, professional staff workers, congregational officers, church council members, and board members will gain insights and best practices for more effective leadership of their churches. The book is also an appropriate primer on congregational organization for students preparing for parish ministry"-- Provided by publisher.

Identifiers: LCCN 2022025433 (print) | LCCN 2022025434 (ebook) | ISBN 9780758673114 (paperback) | ISBN 9780758673121 (ebook)

Subjects: LCSH: Church management.

Classification: LCC BV652 .P49 2023 (print) | LCC BV652 (ebook) | DDC 254--dc23/eng/20221228

LC record available at https://lccn.loc.gov/2022025433

LC ebook record available at https://lccn.loc.gov/2022025434

---

3 4 5 6 7 8 9 10 11 12 32 31 30 29 28 27 26 25 24 23

PRAISE FOR *ORGANIZING FOR MINISTRY AND MISSION*

Dr. Peter has done a marvelous job in *Organizing for Ministry and Mission,* laying out for congregations important and needed information on organizational life and operations. He lays out clear methods for congregations as they operate and organize themselves. This information is especially helpful for congregational leaders and administrators as they carry out the task of keeping the ministry moving forward. He does a masterful job at maintaining the importance of Word and Sacrament ministry as the heart and soul of any congregational life and organization. This is a must-read for all congregational leaders and pastors.

Rev. Dr. Jamison Hardy,
president and bishop of the English District,
assistant pastor of Our Savior Lutheran Church, Hartland, Michigan

---

We're saved by grace, not by enduring endless, boring meetings. The Holy Spirit gathers and nurtures us, not constitutions, bylaws, and budgets. Still, earthly practices help make the mission of God incarnate to us and through us to our neighborhoods and communities. From my experience, good governance is often neglected in many—I'm afraid in most—churches. David Peter's work, solidly theological, offers an opportunity for honest reflection on how effectively we are, or are not, functioning. I suggest my fellow pastors consider reading through this helpful book with their congregational leadership.

Dale A. Meyer,
president emeritus, Concordia Seminary

Frustration. Wasted time. Lack of direction. Too many positions to fill. What kind of structure is best for your congregation? Can things get better organizationally in your congregation? Yes, someone is listening and responding to the real dilemmas that congregations and leaders are facing. David Peter responds to these concerns and more in *Organizing for Ministry and Mission.* As you read this book, you will gain biblical and theological insights, options for growing an impactful organization, and true hope for a well-run congregation rooted in Christ and ready for His mission. There is no despair in this book, only confidence that Christ is at work, and will continue to be at work. It is filled with practical ideas for you and your congregation to consider, including how to raise up new leaders for service. If you are looking for less frustrating meetings, more rich and clear congregational life, and especially stronger ministry and mission, this is the book for you!

Rev. Dr. Allan R. Buss,
president, Northern Illinois District

David Peter has written the definite resource on board governance for congregations. *Organizing for Ministry and Mission* adroitly acknowledges that each church is unique in culture, history, size, and programmatic complexity and, as such, one governance model does not fit all. Peter combines a theological framework with a practical approach that allows a congregation's governance model to addition of value to its mission as opposed to an exercise in frustration. A "how to" guide for every seminarian and a must read for all of us who are lay leaders and pastors in our churches.

Dr. Kurt Senske,
author, *The CEO and the Board: The Art of Nonprofit Governance as a Competitive Advantage*, founder and principal of CEO-Board Services.

David Peter does an excellent job making the case for the importance and necessity of a congregation giving attention to its organizational structure as it serves the essence of the Church—the Gospel of Jesus Christ. Congregations will benefit from this book, as it provides a wealth of information useful for every congregation, regardless of size or context. As the leader of the Post-Seminary Applied Learning and Support (PALS) program, I will definitely recommend this book to new pastors transitioning into their first call.

Rev. Dr. James A. Baneck,
executive director of pastoral education,
The Lutheran Church—Missouri Synod

David Peter provides a compelling case that since God is a God of order and His very creation exhibits organization, so should God's Church be as it carries out God's mission. While insisting that organization is not optional, Peter does not insist on a one-size-fits-all approach. He provides a theological framework for organizing the local congregation and presents the three most common approaches in organizing congregations today, weighing the strengths and weaknesses of each. This book is a valuable resource for those who wish to examine their own congregational structure, especially as changes in context occur.

Rev. Dr. Glen Thomas,
senior pastor, St. Paul's Lutheran Church and School,
St. Louis, Missouri

CONTENTS

Acknowledgments 1

PART I: The Need for Organization in the Church 2

CHAPTER 1: Organization Is Not Optional 5

Ministry Requires Organization. 6

Organizing after the Exodus 7

Organizing God's People in the Scriptures 8

Organism or Organization? 10

Contextual Considerations 12

The Means, not the End 12

Options, but not Optional 15

CHAPTER 2: A Theological Framework for Organizing Congregations 17

We Start with the Articles 18

The Spiritual Dimension of the Church 20

The Sociological Dimension of the Church 23

Implications of the Two Dimensions 24

One for the Other 26

Distinguished but not Neglected. 27

Latitude in Using Organizational Structures 29

Summary 30

CHAPTER 3: Congregational Organization Exemplified: Walther's Proper Form of a Lutheran Congregation 33

Putting the Priorities into Practice 36

Searching for Structure 39

Takeaways for Today 42

Summary 44

PART II: Options for Organization in the Church 46

CHAPTER 4: The Working Board: The Traditional Model of Church Organization 49

Getting to Work 49

A Simple Structure for the Small Congregation 50

A Complex Structure for the Medium and Large Church 51

Advantages of the Working Board Model 54

— Just Do It 54

— Easy Apprehension 54

— Perpetuating Established Priorities 55

— Promotion of Participation 55

Challenges of the Working Board Model 56

— Neglect of a Unified Strategic Direction 56

— Mired in Meetings 57

— Demand on Human Resources 57

Weighing the Value of the Working Board Option . . 58

CHAPTER 5: The Managing Board: The Streamlined Model of Church Organization 61

Hands Off and On 61

Constituting a Managing Board 62

Integrating Professional Staff 64

The Apprentice 65

Advantages of the Managing Board Model 67

— Accommodation of Ad Hoc Involvement 67

— Streamlined and Simple 68

— Leadership Formation 68

— A Strategic Voice 68

— Adaptability to a Staff-Run Church 69

Challenges of the Managing Board Model 69

— Unqualified Lay Directors 70

— Finding the Time 71

— Keeping Hands Off 71

— Management becomes Maintenance 71
— Disharmony 72
— Addressing the Perils 73
Weighing the Value of the Managing Board Option 74

CHAPTER 6: The Governing Board: The Corporate Model of Church Organization 77
Distinctive Characteristics of a Governing Board . . . 78
Governing through Policies 80
— Ends Policies 80
— Limitations Policies 81
— Linkage and Process Policies 81
Executing the Policies 82
Advantages of the Governing Board Model 85
— Clear Lines of Accountability 85
— Clear Roles and Responsibilities 86
— Separation of Governance from Operations 87
— Coordinated Design 87
— Freedom within Boundaries 88
Challenges of the Governing Board Model 89
— The Need for Paid Staff 89
— Discontented Staff 90
— Holding Volunteers Accountable 91
— The Lacuna of Leadership 92
— The Secular CEO Syndrome 93
— Board Member Malaise 94

Weighing the Value of the Governing Board Model 96

PART III: Improving Organization in the Church 98

CHAPTER 7: Developing Action Teams 101
Anatomy of an Action Team 102
Added Value 103

How the Three Models Use Action Teams 105
— Working Board Application 105
— Managing Board Application 106
— Governing Board Application. 107
Forming Action Teams 109
Summary. 111

CHAPTER 8: Forming Competent Board Leaders 113
Equipping Lay Leaders 113
Instruction. 114
Instruction Applied to Organizational Models. . . . 116
Immersion 119
Immersion Applied to Organizational Models 120
— Working Board Application 120
— Managing Board Application 120
— Governing Board Application. 121
Imitation 122
Imitation Applied to Organizational Models 124
— Working Board Application 124
— Managing Board Application 125
— Governing Board Application. 126
Summary. 127

CHAPTER 9: Empowering Innovative Board Leaders 131
Empowerment 132
Innovation. 133
Application to Organizational Models 137
Innovate by Addressing Problems 137
Innovate by Addressing Products 139
Innovate by Addressing Processes. 140
Summary. 141

CHAPTER 10: Integrating Spiritual Practices into Board Business 143

Devoting Time 145

The Spiritual Practice of Learning 147

— Practices to Promote Learning: Studying God's Word 149

• Bible Study 150

• Study of Spiritual Literature 151

The Spiritual Practice of Sharing 153

— Practices to Promote Sharing: Telling Stories of God's Work. 155

• Stories of God's Work to You. 157

• Stories of God's Work through You 157

• Stories of God's Work Witnessed by Recipients 158

The Spiritual Practice of Praying 159

— Practices to Promote Praying: Talking to God 161

• Scheduled Prayers 161

• Formal Prayers 162

• Spontaneous Prayers. 164

Summary. 165

Epilogue 167

APPENDIXES 170

APPENDIX ONE: The Congregation's Constitution and Bylaws. . 173

What Is a Constitution? 174

What Are Bylaws? 175

Why Are the Constitution and Bylaws Needed? . . 176

How Are the Constitution and Bylaws Developed? 178

Conclusion. 179

APPENDIX TWO: Organizational Charts 181

What Is an Organizational Chart? 181

Why Is an Organizational Chart Needed? 184

Who Is Included in an Organizational Chart? 185

How Is an Organizational Chart Developed? 186

Conclusion. 188

Sample Organizational Chart: African Immigrant Ministry, Mount Zion Church, Anytown 188

ACKNOWLEDGMENTS

I am indebted to many for the insights offered in this book. I gained much understanding of organization dynamics in a large church during a decade of pastoral ministry at Trinity Lutheran Church in Peoria, Illinois. I have also become familiar with the distinctive ways that small churches organize by serving St. John Lutheran Church in St. James, Missouri.

In my role as a seminary professor, I have learned much about how different congregations organize as I teach courses in parish administration and pastoral leadership. It is said that the best way to learn something is to teach it, and that certainly applies to me. In and out of the classroom, I have gained many insights about the theology, theory, and practice of parish ministry from my students and faculty colleagues. Lastly, I have come to deepen my understanding of organization in congregations from the true practitioners of parish administration—my fellow pastors.

PART I

THE NEED FOR ORGANIZATION IN THE CHURCH

When it comes to the mission and ministry of the Church, organizational details are not the main thing. Congregational leaders—pastors, church staff, laity—are more concerned about connecting the Gospel with people, and rightly so. These leaders prioritize the accomplishment of the Great Commission and the demonstration of the Great Commandment. These leaders aspire to be ministers of the Word more than marshals of the workers.

Yet if the mission and ministry of the Church are to advance forward, leaders need to give attention to matters of organization. This is because mission and ministry are about people—people to be formed in faith and sent in service. And the processes of formation and sending involve organization. The saints need to be mobilized and managed.

Patrick Lencioni, a highly regarded writer on leadership dynamics, maintains that organizational health is the foremost advantage that any corporate institution has in accomplishing its mission. He asserts that successful companies are distinguished most from unsuccessful ones by how effectively they organize.[1] When it comes to the Church, of course, there are other factors at play in what brings about success—most notably theological and spiritual variables. But even for the Church, organizational health makes a big difference.

Although leaders may not relish matters of administration, organizing the work of the Church is necessary. It is needed because God has hardwired order in His creation. In the very beginning, God created the heavens and the earth in an orderly manner (Genesis 1). We observe amazing order in the structures of molecules and the patterns of galaxies. So also, human beings, created to be social

1 Patrick Lencioni, *The Advantage: Why Organizational Health Trumps Everything Else in Business* (Hoboken, NJ: John Wiley, 2012), 8–9.

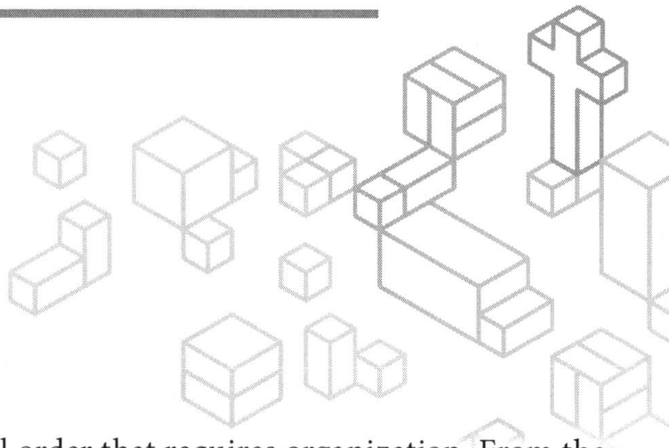

creatures, live in a social order that requires organization. From the family unit to national governments, organization is necessary for humans to flourish.

The functioning of the Church also requires order. Certainly, there is *theological* order: Christ is the head of His Body, the Church (Ephesians 1:22–23). But *social* order is also needed in Christian congregations. Because we now live in a broken creation, marred by sin, no social order will be perfect. But that doesn't mean that organization isn't necessary. Nor does it mean that organizing a church cannot bear rich fruit for advancing God's purposes for His people. In fact, attention to organizational matters can improve the functioning of a church's ministry and mission. Organization is not the essence of the Church's work, but it can be beneficial to the Church's work.

Part 1 of this book investigates why organization is needed in Christian congregations. Three chapters present the rationale for church organization. Chapter 1 argues that organization isn't optional for congregations, so pastors and leaders do well to give it thoughtful attention in ministry. Chapter 2 offers a theological framework for congregational organization as it envisions the Church within two dimensions. Chapter 3 demonstrates how a work by Dr. Carl F. W. Walther, a prominent theologian in the American Lutheran Church, puts these principles into practice. These chapters will hopefully inspire you to value the task of organization in your church and then execute that task with theological integrity and missional productivity.

When it comes to the mission and ministry of the Church, organizational details are not the main thing, but they are something. They are important. They are necessary. We investigate the reasons why in this opening section.

CHAPTER 1

ORGANIZATION **IS NOT** OPTIONAL

Ryan Clemens was frustrated. In his role as congregational president of Mount Zion Church, he had become convinced that the people who served on the church's boards were not performing to their potential. These boards comprised the organizational structure of the church. Ryan believed that the structure itself was partly to blame for hindering the congregation's efforts to move forward in ministry and mission.

The laypeople who filled the boards overseeing the ministry efforts of Mount Zion Church were for the most part committed to their responsibilities. The boards made possible an ongoing execution of the areas of ministry that the church identified as priorities—worship, education, youth, children, service, and outreach. Yet this system was not efficient. It did not produce the results that Ryan had hoped for during his current two-year stint as council president. Ryan wasn't convinced that this organizational structure facilitated the best stewardship of the time, energy, gifts, and efforts of its participants.

Ryan was concerned that a disproportionate amount of time was spent by the elected board members in meetings instead of in action. During these meetings, they discussed the church's needs and offered proposals to address those needs. But at subsequent meetings, the participants simply reported on what had transpired to advance these proposals, and it usually wasn't much. Then they would rehash much of the previous meetings' discussion. These boards met monthly, in accordance with the bylaws, whether they needed to or not.

Ryan became convinced that many of these church meetings dealt with issues that should have been simply delegated to individuals or small teams rather than be discussed in detail by standing boards. He once commented to another church leader: "We are good at taking lots of minutes and wasting lots of hours." And Ryan's frustration was shared by others. Increasingly, the directors found it difficult to get the other members of their boards to attend meetings. The nominating committee had a hard go of it in recruiting volunteers to serve on the boards. Sometimes less competent candidates were nominated for positions simply to fill the required slots on the election slate. The church's core value of parishioner participation was increasingly at risk.

Ryan contemplated his service as congregational president, and while he did so, certain questions emerged in his mind: Are there other options for organizing the church's formal board structure so that greater efficiency, effectiveness, and fruitfulness may result? How can Mount Zion Church be better organized so that corporately it is a good steward of the time, talents, and resources of its lay participants? All this compelled Ryan to consider a far more fundamental question: Is an organizational structure even necessary to carry out the mission and ministry of Mount Zion Church?

MINISTRY REQUIRES ORGANIZATION

The local congregation develops ministry efforts to accomplish God's mandate. These initiatives intend to bring God's gracious presence to people through His Word of the Gospel (Ephesians 1:3–14). They aim to deliver God's power to release people from the bondage of sin and to enable sanctified living (Ephesians 1:15–2:10). They undertake to execute God's plan of reconciliation (Ephesians 2:11–22). They seek to promote maturation of the saints (Ephesians 4:1–16). Such efforts, when aligned with these priorities, accomplish great and marvelous things in this world and for the world to come!

But the development and implementation of these ministry activities do not occur automatically and without effort. They require very intentional thinking and acting. Since they are done collaboratively, they require organization. Participation by multiple people in a shared effort will require some degree of organization. This is done so that the work of the Church is conducted effectively.

Unfortunately, organizing a congregation is rarely easy. Ryan Clemens experienced this firsthand at Mount Zion Church. Such challenges are not uncommon. Many congregations struggle to find the right approach or structure for organizing their efforts. The appropriate organizational model can contribute to fruitful mission and ministry. A faulty organizational structure can lead to frustration and failure.

ORGANIZING AFTER THE EXODUS

Ryan Clemens is not the first person to be frustrated with the way things were operating in his congregation. An early book of the Bible depicts a similar scene involving a man appointed to lead God's people.

Moses was exhausted and frustrated. In fact, he was about to burn out! There was exasperation in his voice. Moreover, the people he was called to lead were upset and impatient with him. Things did not look good for Moses' ministry among the Israelites.

You might suspect that this describes what Moses encountered after years of wandering in the wilderness with the cantankerous and complaining mob. However, this troubling situation arose only a few months after the exodus from Egypt. The Israelites were near Mount Sinai, where Moses was to meet with God, yet he found himself surrounded by folks clamoring for his attention. The Bible says that "the people stood around Moses from morning till evening" waiting for him to attend to their needs (Exodus 18:13).

Fortunately, God sent an objective outsider to assess the situation and give helpful guidance. Moses' father-in-law, Jethro, arrived from Midian and was astounded at what he observed. "What is this that you are doing for the people?" Jethro interjected. "What you are doing is not good. You and the people with you will certainly wear yourselves out, for the thing is too heavy for you. You are not able to do it alone" (Exodus 18:14, 17–18).

Jethro then offered a solution to his son-in-law's dilemma. Moses was to select capable, faith-filled, and trustworthy men and delegate some of his responsibilities to them. This would lighten the load for

Moses and would multiply the ministry among others. But Jethro didn't stop there with his recommendation. He proposed that Moses *organize* these assistants into a system of oversight and accountability. Jethro advised to "place such men over the people as chiefs of thousands, of hundreds, of fifties, and of tens" (Exodus 18:21). This is a clear and orderly *organizational structure.*

Moses heeded the advice of his father-in-law, as the text reports: "Moses chose able men out of all Israel and made them heads over the people, chiefs of thousands, of hundreds, of fifties, and of tens. And they judged the people at all times" (Exodus 18:25–26). Here we see a decimal division organized in a pyramidal structure. It forms a pattern of delegated responsibility with a line of accountability. Most importantly, it solved the problem of backlog for the needs of the people, and it prevented the burnout of their primary leader.

The result, as Jethro had promised, was relief and effective ministry: "You will be able to endure, and all these people also will go to their place in peace" (Exodus 18:23). What had been a lose-lose situation (the people upset and the leader exhausted) was transformed into a win-win phenomenon (the leader is renewed, and the people are satisfied), all because of attention to organizational structure.

ORGANIZING GOD'S PEOPLE IN THE SCRIPTURES

The narrative of Moses organizing others to assist him in leading the people is representative of many stories from the Bible that illustrate the need to organize God's people. In the Old Testament, we read of Abraham organizing a posse to rescue his nephew Lot (Genesis 14:1–16). Joseph organized a food-relief program that preserved Jacob's family through famine (Genesis 41:33–42:5). Joshua organized a campaign to conquer and settle the Promised Land (Joshua 6–21). Deborah organized a resistance force against invading foreigners (Judges 4). David organized an effective government as well as worship leadership (1 Chronicles 23–27). Solomon organized an economic system that brought prosperity to his kingdom (2 Chronicles 8–9). Daniel's organizational skill elevated him to a high office in the administration of a world empire (Daniel 6:1–3). Haggai and Zechariah inspired the post-exilic community of Judahites to rebuild the temple (Ezra 5:1–2; Haggai 1; Zechariah 1). Nehemiah mobilized the inhabitants of Jerusalem to rebuild the city walls (Nehemiah 2–6). Esther and Mordecai organized a plan to deliver the Jews from annihilation (Esther 4:12–17).

This need for organization continues in the New Testament. It was evident in the Early Church. The distribution of resources by the Jerusalem Church required organization that evolved according to the needs of the situation (Acts 4:32–37; 6:1–7). The spread of the mission to the Gentiles required organized effort and accountability (Acts 11:1–30; 13:1–3; 15:1–35). The apostle Paul exhorted the Corinthian Christians to conduct worship in an orderly manner, which implies some degree of organization in the worship service (1 Corinthians 14:26–40). He also organized a fund-raising effort to aid the poor Christians in Jerusalem (2 Corinthians 8–9). In the Pastoral Epistles, Paul exhorts Timothy and Titus to give attention to the organizational needs of their respective congregations (1 Timothy 5:1–25; Titus 1:5–11).

These narratives illustrate how God used leaders to organize His people according to His purposes. Moreover, organization requires structure. There must be a design that is understandable, orderly, and replicable. The organizational structure depicted in Exodus exemplifies this: "chiefs of thousands, of hundreds, of fifties, and of tens" (Exodus 18:25). Occasionally the scriptural accounts report how an organizational effort was structured (e.g., Numbers 2:1–34; 10:11–36; Judges 7:15–18; 1 Chronicles 24–27). Usually in Scripture, the precise designs of organizational structure are not described in detail. This indicates that the specific details of organization are distinctive to a given context and thus are not prescriptive for all occasions or settings. But the need to organize is shared by all social units, including Christian congregations. In this regard, organization is not optional for churches today.

Congregations do well to organize into structures that distribute the labor and facilitate a broad participation of members. The desired outcome is not the perpetuation of a bureaucracy but that all things are "done decently and in order" (1 Corinthians 14:40). Another goal of the organizational structure is that people's gifts and abilities are optimally engaged. Ultimately, this is for the purpose of attending to God's priorities for His Church. Administrative structures are tools for achieving the goals of the congregation; they serve to advance the mission of God.

ORGANISM OR ORGANIZATION?

Most churches offer ministry efforts, missional initiatives, and service projects that take the form of programs. This programmatic design necessitates organizational structures. Usually such structures involve boards, committees, and teams to oversee and implement the programs.

It is not uncommon for people who are involved with these church boards and committees to become frustrated, as Ryan Clemens was in the account narrated earlier. These folks discover that administration and organization dominate much of the time and energy of the ministry effort. Like Ryan, they lament that the meetings cause them to "take minutes and waste hours." They begin to feel strangled with institutionalism.

Understandably, these leaders search for alternative options. They seek to make the congregation function less bureaucratically and more fluidly. They attempt to transform the structure of the church to become more organic and less institutional. They aspire to see that the energy of the whole is invested more into ministry impact rather than in administrative maintenance. These instincts are usually well founded, and the efforts commendable.

Yet there ever exists the pull toward organizational structure, especially as a church increases in membership and complexity. How is this tension resolved between the Church's identity as an organism—the Body of Christ—and its composition as an organization? How does a congregation reconcile the paradox that it is composed of a spiritual priesthood as well as of human creatures who work together under institutional rules, expectations, and policies?

Jim Belcher describes his experience as a pastor leading a church plant. When the church grew to a significant size, its social complexity also increased. Belcher describes how, in the first several years after the church was planted, its organization was very organic, even intuitive.

They kept the structure simple, avoiding any encroachment of institutionalism. Nevertheless, Belcher narrates what eventually developed:

> But as we grew, an interesting thing happened. We found that people were getting frustrated with the lack of structure. It may have been organic, but the church seemed too loose, a little too sloppy. When a meeting got canceled for a good reason, I thought we were being fluid and flexible. When the church service was not micromanaged, I thought it showed we were spiritual and were trusting God. But some thought otherwise. And the lack of organization made it difficult for newcomers to know how to get involved.
>
> Because of these concerns and all the new growth, we began to initiate more structure. We put together a flow chart of all the different teams, who was leading them and how they related to one another. We had monthly meetings and other planning times. We called our new desire to organize "functional structures."[2]

This resulted in an awkward tension. Some members appreciated more structure, others feared that the church was becoming too institutionalized. But Belcher's quest led him to embrace a balance between the organic nature of the church and its need for organizational structures. He came to understand that it isn't either-or, but both-and. The Christian congregation is both an institution and a living reality, both an organization and an organism. There is not only a spiritual dimension to congregational life. There is an institutional one as well. To avoid or neglect this organizational dynamic will be to the detriment of the Church.[3]

---

2 Jim Belcher, *Deep Church: A Third Way Beyond Emerging and Traditional* (Downers Grove, IL: IVP Books, 2009), 163–64.

3 Timothy Keller capably analyzes this "both-and" nature of the local congregation in a chapter entitled "The Church as an Organized Organism" in *Center Church: Doing Balanced, Gospel-Centered Ministry in Your City* (Grand Rapids: Zondervan, 2012), 344–53.

CONTEXTUAL CONSIDERATIONS

Congregations of all sizes require some form of administrative structure. I have served as the pastor of a small church, a midsize church, and a large church. In each case, organizational structure was evident, but in different forms. Whatever the size, a parish needs structure for there to be order in the operations.

The *form* of structure differs, depending on the context. Thus, the administrative structure in a small church will likely be different from that of a midsize one, as was evident in Pastor Belcher's description of how the structure of his church changed as the congregation grew. But even among congregations that share a similar-size culture, there can be many approaches to organization.

It is up to each congregation to determine what organizational structure will best serve its needs in its distinctive context, as long as that structure conforms to sound theological principles. One church's context may commend a more hierarchical model, while a more flattened structure may be appropriate in a different context. A large church may function best with a staff-led model, whereas a few lay volunteers may comprise the structure of a very small congregation.

Contextual factors come into play when organizing the working arrangements of the church's officers and volunteers. These contextual variables include the size of the congregation, the socio-political makeup of its members, the educational background of the parishioners, and their experiences of organization and leadership in their vocations. Whatever the case, context is an important consideration in designing the governance structure of a church.

THE MEANS, NOT THE END

It is important to recognize, however, that an organizational structure is not an end in itself. An administrative structure exists not merely to perpetuate its own existence, although in this sinful world it can sometimes degenerate to this. (A symptom of this condition is the maintenance-mode bureaucracy evident in some church administrations.) Instead, a structure should be a *means* to accomplish the purposes and priorities God has entrusted to the Church. It is meant to advance the strategic objectives of a congregation as it seeks to carry out God's calling. Ultimately, the organizational structure plays a ministerial role to the magisterial goal of making disciples of Jesus Christ through the teaching of the Gospel.

Colin Marshall employs an image to compare the relationship between the Gospel ministry and the organizational structure of a congregation: a living vine and the trellis that it grows upon. Using this analogy, he writes:

> The basic work of any Christian ministry is to preach the gospel of Jesus Christ in the power of God's Spirit, and to see people converted, changed and grow to maturity in that gospel. That's the work of planting, watering, fertilizing and tending the vine.
>
> However, just as some sort of framework is needed to help a vine grow, so Christian ministries also need some structure and support. It may not be much, but at the very least we need somewhere to meet, some Bibles to read from, and some basic structures of leadership within our group. All Christian churches, fellowships or ministries have some kind of trellis that gives shape and support to the work. As the ministry grows, the trellis also needs attention. Management, finances, infrastructure, organization, governance—these all become more important and more complex as the vine grows. In this sense, good trellis workers are invaluable, and all growing ministries need them.[4]

The Church is a living organism, the Body of Christ. Jesus Himself used the metaphor of the vine and branches to describe His relationship to the members of the Church (John 15:1–11). This is where true life and fruitfulness is. Just as a grapevine will thrive and produce more when it is supported by a trellis, so also the Church of Jesus Christ is supported in its work by the structures of organization and administration.

---

4 Marshall, Collin and Tony Payne, *The Trellis and the Vine: The Ministry Mind-shift that Changes Everything* (Sydney: Matthias Media, 2009), 8.

One of my hobbies is vegetable gardening. One summer, I conducted an experiment in horticulture. I planted two tomato plants next to each other. They were of the same variety and were provided the same conditions of sunlight, soil cultivation, and watering. One plant I trained to grow on a trellis. The other I allowed to creep along the ground without any external support. The difference in fruitfulness was astounding! The vine that was supported on the metal frame bore tomatoes in abundance. The one left unsupported was much less fruitful, and the tomatoes it produced usually spoiled on the ground before ripening. The existence of an inorganic structure (trellis) made a significant difference in how well the organic tomato plants produced fruit.

I have observed a similar dynamic in churches. The congregation is enlivened by the Holy Spirit working through Word and Sacrament. Yet churches that implement organizational structure to support spiritual nurture usually produce more fruit—that is, better mission and ministry—than congregations that don't. There is a need to attend to both the organic (life in the Spirit) and the organizational.

Yet we must remember that the trellis isn't the main thing. The vine is! The viticulturist gives attention to the trellis for the sake of the health and fruitfulness of the vine. Likewise, pastors and congregational leaders will attend to the church's organization for the sake of its Gospel ministry. One serves the other. The trellis supports the vine, not vice versa. And organizational structures serve Gospel ministry. Yet these structures are not the Church's reason to exist.

A congregation is at liberty to choose what form of administrative structure will most benefit the advancement of its purposes and priorities, as long as that structure supports God's will as revealed in His Word. This book will investigate some options for organizational structures that you as a church leader can consider. It will identify some possible models for organizing the lay leaders and the boards and programs they oversee. You will need to use spiritual discernment and sanctified reasoning to decide which model (or synthesis of models) fits best the context and culture of your congregation as it carries out Christ's Great Commission. What follows will provide you with a broader understanding of possibilities for organizing your congregation as well as opportunities to improve its impact.

OPTIONS, BUT NOT OPTIONAL

This book seeks to familiarize you with options for organizing your congregation. But that does not mean that organizational structures are optional in the sense of opting out of organizing altogether. It is not an option as to *if* you will organize. Every congregation requires some organization! The options have to do with *how* you organize. Since a Christian congregation involves a plurality of people working together, there is the need to organize. That is not optional. How it organizes is another matter, and an important one. It may organize itself well or poorly. It is hoped that this resource will equip you to organize your congregation well so that it is productive toward the purposes that God has for it.

CHAPTER 2

A THEOLOGICAL **FRAMEWORK** FOR **ORGANIZING CONGREGATIONS**

In thinking about organizational structures for a congregation, you—as a church leader— may ask: So what does this have to do with *theology*? What does designing organizational charts, developing programs, and coordinating boards and committees have to do with God and His plan of redemption? These are very relevant questions because theology is eminently important, especially when it comes to the ministry and mission of the Church.

Nonetheless, many of these seemingly nontheological tasks—such as organizing human resources and managing people—are necessary for effective ministry. This becomes clear when congregations are not organized or administered well. Participants in ministry become frustrated and disengaged with the church. People turn away from congregations that are poorly managed.

The reality is that the activity of organizing people for mission and ministry has a theological dimension. God is active and involved in it. The reason for this is the pattern God designed in creation. God has ordered the world so that things function differently in different contexts. That includes the distinctive context of a Christian congregation. Attending to the organization of a congregation, which involves attention to management, programs, structure, and staff, is a theological endeavor as one attends to advancing God's mission in the realm of God's creation. We are placed into the pattern of sociological dynamics that ultimately derive from the ways in which God has created human beings to relate and interact with one another. And these differ depending on the context of the social organization, impacting even the ways in which mission and ministry are conducted in congregations of varying sizes and locations.

The chapters in parts 2 and 3 of this book, which present models and practices for organizing congregations, may appear not to be theological at first glance. Matters of theology are not immediately self-evident. Nevertheless, theology remains central to the discussion of this book. It remains vital but in a less evident manner. This chapter will clarify the theological dynamics at work in parish organization.

WE START WITH THE ARTICLES

The most familiar Christian creeds are the Apostles' and Nicene Creeds. Both of these confessional statements are organized into a tripartite structure, and each of the three parts in this structure is referred to as an article. An article focuses on the person and work of one member of the Trinity. Each article presents a concise confession of the essentials regarding faith in one of the persons who constitute the triune God.

The First Article of the Apostles' Creed states very succinctly, "I believe in God, the Father Almighty, maker of heaven and earth." The Nicene Creed adds to this formula: "and of all things visible and invisible."[5] Clearly, then, this article is about the First Person of the Trinity, God the Father, and His creative work. The claim that the Father is "maker of heaven and earth" assumes that He is also the one who sustains and preserves His creation as well as provides for and protects His creatures.

Thus, the primary concern of the First Article is creation. This is significant for our consideration of organizational structures in that the theology of creation informs the design and functioning of social units such as congregations. A prime location in the schema of theological

5 *Concordia: The Lutheran Confessions*, Second edition. (St. Louis: Concordia Publishing House, 2006), 16.

truth for the subject of this book is in the First Article.[6] Insights from the social sciences that align with Scripture and inform the workings of an organization such as a Christian congregation can be regarded as First Article insights.

Yet the purpose of the Church, and thus of individual congregations that compose the Church, is focused in the Second and Third Articles of the Creed. The Church's purpose is to proclaim Jesus Christ, the Son of God, who (according to the Second Article) descended to earth and was incarnated as a human being; He lived, died, rose from the dead, ascended into heaven, and will return again—all "for us men and for our salvation."[7] The goal of this proclamation is that sinful people will believe in Christ and receive the salvation He has procured for them.

This is made possible by the work of the Holy Spirit, whom the Third Article of the Nicene Creed identifies as "the Lord and Giver of Life."[8] He engenders faith in Jesus Christ and delivers the forgiveness of sins through the Gospel, thus imparting eternal life. He gathers the redeemed into the communion of saints, which is the Holy Church. The Spirit "proceeds from the Father and the Son"[9] to distribute through His Word the gifts of life and salvation for this world and the world to come. The Christian Church participates in this mission to reconcile and restore fallen humanity as it is sent in the name of Christ and in the power of the Holy Spirit (Matthew 28:18–20; Luke 24:46–49; John 20:21–23; 2 Corinthians 5:16–21).

This is the purpose of the Church, located squarely in the Second and Third Articles. But this does not mean that matters of the First Article are irrelevant to the mission of God through His Church. Indeed, the ultimate result of the redeeming work of the Son and the regenerative work of the Spirit is the restoration of the entire creation. The three articles are not disintegrated but intersect and interact to accomplish the triune God's saving plan. This means that insights from the First Article should serve and support the redemptive mission of

6 The identification of categorical *locations* for doctrinal truth is a traditional practice in the field of doctrinal or systematic theology. Indeed, the technical word used by theologians is *locus*, the Latin word for "place" or "location."

7 *Concordia: The Lutheran Confessions,* 16.

8 *Concordia: The Lutheran Confessions,* 16.

9 *Concordia: The Lutheran Confessions,* 16.

God, which is confessed in the Second and Third Articles of the Creed. Insights about the created order and social organization can promote the faithful and fruitful mission and ministry of God's Church.

This integration of the creaturely character of the Church (First Article) and its spiritual expression (Third Article) is evident in the description of the Church provided in one of the foundational confessional documents of the evangelical faith, the Apology of the Augsburg Confession. This Confession, forged out of the struggle of the Reformation, states: "But the Church is not only the fellowship of outward objects and rites, as other governments, but at its core, it is a fellowship of faith and of the Holy Spirit in hearts."[10] This statement identifies two dimensions of the Church—a sociological one "as other governments" (First Article), and a spiritual one—"a fellowship of faith and of the Holy Spirit" (Third Article). We will now take a closer look at each of these two dimensions of the Church.[11]

THE SPIRITUAL DIMENSION OF THE CHURCH

We begin with the spiritual dimension of the Church because that is the focus and emphasis of this section of the Apology, which states that this dimension is what the Church is at its core. The Church in its essence is the association of people brought to saving faith by the power of the Holy Spirit. The article continues to identify the marks of the Church in this dimension: "These marks are the pure doctrine of the Gospel and the administration of the Sacraments in accordance with the Gospel of Christ."[12] The Apology identifies this Church with Christ's body: "This Church alone is called Christ's body, which Christ renews, sanctifies, and governs by His Spirit."[13] These

10 Ap VII and VIII 5.

11 I am indebted to Charles Arand for articulating these dimensions of the Church. What I write here follows closely his treatment of these dimensions in "The Ministry of the Church in Light of the Two Kinds of Righteousness," *Concordia Journal* 33:4 (Fall 2007), 344–56; and "Living in Two Worlds: The Challenge of Church and Ministry in the Twenty-First Century" (unpublished essay, 2014).

12 Ap VII and VIII 5.

13 Ap VII and VIII 5.

words indicate that the Apology views the Church primarily through the lens of the Third Article. In fact, the author, Philip Melanchthon, locates this dimension of the Church accordingly.

> The Church is defined by the Third Article of the Creed, which teaches us to believe that there is a holy Catholic Church. . . . The words that follow, namely, "the communion of saints," seems to be added in order to explain what the Church signifies: the congregation of saints, who have with each other the fellowship of the same Gospel or doctrine and the same Holy Spirit, who renews, sanctifies, and governs their hearts.[14]

Several truths are affirmed in this confession of the Church. First, in the spiritual dimension, the Church is envisioned as an organism more than as an organization. The Church is a living entity, the Body of Christ, which is enlivened by the Spirit of God. There exists a mystical union between Christ and the baptized so that they are in Christ (Romans 8:1; Galatians 3:26–28; Philippians 1:1; 1 Peter 5:14) and He is in them (Luke 17:21; John 6:56; Romans 8:10; Colossians 1:27).

Second, the spiritual dimension of the Church can be viewed only through the eyes of faith. The Christian confesses in the Creed, "I *believe* in the Holy Spirit, the holy Christian Church, the communion of saints."[15] And what is in view is faith itself, which cannot be seen by human eyes. The Church is, as the Apology expresses it, "a fellowship of faith and of the Holy Spirit in hearts."[16] This is how God sees the Church. It is the Church *coram deo*, before God.

Nevertheless, even though faith cannot be empirically assessed in people, one may still perceive the visible Means of Grace that enliven faith in congregations. Thus, the Apology continues its description of the Church in the spiritual dimension: "These marks are the pure doctrine of the Gospel and the administration of the Sacraments in accordance with the Gospel of Christ."[17] Christian pastors and

---

14 Ap VII and VIII 7–8.

15 *Concordia: The Lutheran Confessions*, 16. Emphasis mine.

16 Ap VII and VIII 5

17 Ap VII and VIII 5.

the congregations they lead are therefore to give highest priority to faithfully preaching and teaching God's Word and to baptizing and distributing the Lord's Supper.

Third, Christian congregations and their leaders are to attend to these priorities—proclaiming the Gospel and administering the Sacraments—because this is what God has mandated the Church to do. Jesus has assigned to the Church the mission of making disciples by baptizing and teaching His Word (Matthew 28:18–20). Pastors are called to minister publicly the Means of Grace in order to engender, nurture, and sustain faith among God's people (1 Timothy 4:6–16; 2 Timothy 1:13–14; 2:15; 4:1–5; Titus 2:1, 15). In Christ's stead, the Church administers the Keys to His kingdom by proclaiming the message of the Law, which announces God's judgment upon the unrepentant, and the message of the Gospel, which delivers forgiveness of sins to the repentant (Matthew 16:19; 18:18; John 20:22–23). This "special authority which Christ has given to His church on earth"[18] is not optional or open to negotiation. It is *de jure divino,* mandated by divine authority. The responsibilities and duties that Christ has entrusted to His Church and the Holy Spirit enlivens and empowers are essential to the Church's identity and mission. Accordingly, pastors and church leaders do not neglect them but earnestly attend to them.

In short, this spiritual dimension is essentially what the Church is. It is the Church's *esse.* Or to return to the wording of the Apology, "At its core, it is a fellowship of faith and of the Holy Spirit in hearts."[19] The local Christian congregation—its pastors, staff workers, lay leaders, and members—give first priority to the proprium of the Church by proclaiming God's Word of Law and Gospel, by teaching the faith, and by administering the Sacraments according to Christ's command.

18 Small Catechism, Confession, "What is the Office of the Keys?".

19 Ap VII and VIII 5.

THE SOCIOLOGICAL DIMENSION OF THE CHURCH

In addition to the spiritual dimension, there is another manifestation of the Church to which pastors and baptized believers give attention. This is a sociological expression. Note again these words from the Apology: "The Church is not only the fellowship of outward objects and rites, as other governments."[20] This clause states that the Church is like other governments or civic organizations in that it is an association ("fellowship") of external (observable) objects and rites. But it is not only this. The Church is more because it encompasses the spiritual dimension described previously, which other secular organizations such as commercial businesses, government agencies, and nonprofit charities do not. Yet in other regards, the Church certainly *is* like these other governments, like other civic organizations. This is so in its sociological manifestation.

The Apology does not expound on this dimension because it was not a major issue of contention during the Reformation. But the fact that it recognizes this expression of the Church is significant. Church leaders certainly do not neglect its spiritual dimension. But they also do not ignore the Church's sociological manifestation.

The Church is in fact an association. It is "as other governments." It is a fellowship of outward ties in that it is composed of people who associate with one another by way of shared bonds. They have a common purpose and relate to one another via social connections. They also share rites, that is, social performances and practices that bind communities together and advance their goals. In this regard, the Church is "as other governments." Christian congregations share characteristics of other human organizations that are not spiritually oriented. Although churches are not essentially businesses, congregations do need to conduct business. It needs to organize itself to assign roles and distribute responsibilities to its members. It requires leadership and lines of authority. Work must be delegated, managed, and supervised in order to advance the congregation's purpose and goals. This expresses the organizational dynamic, and that is the focus

20 Ap VII and VIII 5.

of this book. As the Apology affirms, the Church is a fellowship, an association. By very definition, associations are social entities (note that *socia* is in the word *association*). Therefore, the Church has a sociological dimension to which leaders give attention.

The relevance of this for the study of congregational organization is that human beings congregate into different social groupings, and these various communities function differently depending on their sizes and context. This is where the social sciences can be of benefit. It is true that some theories proposed by social scientists are incongruent with and even antithetical to the scriptural revelation. Accordingly, the Christian leader uses discernment in employing the social sciences for the sake of Christian ministry and mission. But many of the findings of sociologists and organizational analysts provide useful insights into the created order. The social sciences provide penetrating observations into the intricate and complex interactions among human beings that result from the wondrous ways in which God has created us. It is true that these scientists are observing *sinful* people, and that is not how God originally created us. Yet the interactions of sinful humans can be the target of fruitful investigation and analysis by the social sciences for appropriation to the work of the Church, since the Church ministers to sinners.

IMPLICATIONS OF THE TWO DIMENSIONS

There are several implications of this reality that we do well to consider. First, whereas the spiritual dimension of the Church is its expression according to the Third Article of the Creed, the sociological dimension is the expression of the Church according to the First Article. The primary concern of the First Article is creation. The doctrine of creation informs the design and functioning of social units such as congregations. Accordingly, the location of congregational organization in the schema of theological truth is in the First Article. It concerns First Article theology, which values observation and analysis of the created order, including social order. We glean First Article insights from the social sciences to inform the workings of an organization of human creatures such as a Christian congregation, albeit always with biblical discernment. Thus, even these sociological applications have a theological character in the category of the First Article.

Second, whereas the spiritual dimension envisions the Church as an organism, the Body of Christ, the sociological dimension envisions it as an organization. It is "as other governments," and so can be compared to other organizations in the civil or secular realm. This means that it is beneficial to study social theory and organizational dynamics from the disciplines of sociology, management, organizational leadership, and so forth, and apply these with theological discernment to Christian congregations. Insights about organizational structures, strategic planning, teamwork dynamics, and so forth, which originate in the business world or from political science, may have a salutary application in the congregational context. An example of this, which will be explored later, is the accommodation to churches of policy-based governance originally developed by John Carver and applied to for-profit and not-for-profit corporations.

Third, the sociological expression of the Church is one that is not viewed by the eyes of faith but rather from the natural perspective. This is what the Apology means when it refers to this dimension as involving "outward objects and rites," as opposed to internal faith. Permit me to employ some theological labels using Latin to make this distinction in the next few paragraphs.[21] The sociological expression is not the Church *coram deo* (before God), as with the spiritual dimension. It is the Church *coram mundo* (before the world) or *coram hominibus* (before humans). It is how secular society views churches. For example, the U.S. government views a local Christian congregation as a not-for-profit faith-based organization. The Internal Revenue Service categorizes churches together with other nonprofit groups such as the Red Cross and Habitat for Humanity by granting tax-exempt status. Accordingly, local congregations are subject to the laws and regulations of the state as other organizations are subject. This has special relevance to the focus of this book in that the state may require a congregation to register its constitution and bylaws, which articulate the organizational structure of the congregation.

21 These Latin terms are employed by Charles Arand in the two works to which this chapter is indebted: "The Ministry of the Church in Light of the Two Kinds of Righteousness," and "Living in Two Worlds." They are employed here according to Arand's usage.

Fourth, the spiritual dimension of the Church exists *de jure divino* (by divine design and mandate). However, the sociological dimension is exclusively *de jure humano* (by human design and development). In other words, human beings innovate the various ways of organizing themselves in congregations and execute these as best serve the needs and goals of the Church. The Gospel ministry of the Church is located in the spiritual dimension, and this is not negotiable. But the strategies, methods, and organization for advancing that ministry will vary from context to context according to human design. Congregations may choose from various options for organizing themselves, or they can innovate new options. A significant purpose of this book is to familiarize you with some of these options (see Part 2: Options for Organization in the Church). But the point is that none of these options are mandated by the Lord because they are *de jure humano* and not *de jure divino*.

Finally, the sociological dimension of the Church is not the essence of the Church, theologically speaking. The *esse* (essence) of the Church is found in "the pure doctrine of the Gospel and the administration of the Sacraments,"[22] that is, in the spiritual dimension. Nevertheless, the sociological dimension can and should serve the advancement of the *esse* of the Church. It is *bene esse*—for the good of what is essential. In fact, to neglect the organizational dynamic of a congregation is to hinder its Gospel ministry and mission, since gathering the saints to be nurtured in the Word and Sacraments and mobilizing them for service in God's kingdom requires organization.

ONE FOR THE OTHER

These are the two dimensions of the Church—spiritual and sociological. Both are important. But this doesn't mean that they share equal priority for the life of the Church. Indeed, one dimension serves the other. In the ministry of the Church, the sociological serves the spiritual. The First Article insights are used to advance the Second Article message and the Third Article mission of God. The institutional marks of a congregation—laws of incorporation, organizational structures, constitutional bylaws, church councils, and program boards—serve to

22 Ap VII and VIII 5.

advance the Spirit-wrought marks of the Church—the pure teaching of the Gospel and faithful administration of the Sacraments. Human-designed methods and mechanisms (*de jure humano*) are placed into the service of the divinely mandated mission and ministry (*de jure divino*). Human wisdom submits to divine revelation in the ministerial use of reason. The *bene esse* benefits the *esse.*

Recall the analogy used earlier of the vine and the trellis. The vine is the object of cultivation, and the trellis is a support to it. Similarly, the Gospel ministry of a congregation (the spiritual dimension) should be the focus of its efforts, and the organizational structure (the sociological expression) is developed to serve and support that ministry.

Danger arises when this order is reversed and the trellis becomes the priority over the vine—that is, the sociological manifestation of the Church becomes the priority over the spiritual dimension. Charles Arand describes this error: "At their worst, first article gifts can unintentionally be used to replace or supplant the gospel so that the focus shifts from growing the church as a fellowship of faith to growing the church as a first article organization or institution. This happens by placing more emphasis on first article gifts and goals than third article theology and teaching."[23] Such a development may look impressive in the eyes of the world as the congregation becomes more efficient with lots of professionalism and polish. But if it is devoid of the Spirit working through His Word, it is merely a First Article institution.

Therefore, it is critical to put first things first. The spiritual dimension has a magisterial position, while the sociological dimension plays a ministerial role. Pastor and people in a Christian congregation give attention to First Article matters and organizational dynamics in order to enhance the opportunities for the Holy Spirit to work through Word and Sacrament.

DISTINGUISHED BUT NOT NEGLECTED

This priority given to the spiritual dimension, however, doesn't mean that the sociological issues are unimportant. They are vital to the effective functioning of the Church. They serve a supportive

23 Arand, "Living in Two Worlds," 16.

role to the Church's mission, and to neglect them will result in the hindering of that mission. Both are needed. Although the spiritual and sociological dimensions are to be distinguished, they are not to be separated. Arand observes:

> These two dimensions must remain distinct in order for them to function properly according to God's order and thereby accomplish their purposes. They can be confused in one of two ways, each of which reduces the church to a one-dimensional existence. First, when one equates the organized church with the assembly of saints, and equates organizational growth with the growth of the assembly of saints, one turns the horizontal [sociological] axis into a vertical [spiritual] axis. In these instances, the church as an association of external ties comes to be regarded as coextensive with the church as an assembly of faith. Then works invariably usurp faith. On the other hand, when one focuses exclusively on the church as a spiritual entity and ignores the sociological manifestation of the church, one becomes irrelevant and docetic. Both are important, but for different reasons and different purposes.[24]

The two dimensions of the Church are both distinguished and valued. Pastors and congregational leaders who are wise and faithful to their responsibilities will give due diligence to both. Furthermore, these dimensions are to be integrated so that the sociological dynamics of the Church are informed by biblical truth and the organizational practices are formed by the Word of God. Some organizational practices do not align with sound theology and so are to be eschewed. But pastors and lay leaders can use sanctified discernment guided by the Word of God to organize their congregations in faithful ways to advance the kingdom of God.

24 Arand, "Living in Two Worlds," 6–7.

LATITUDE IN USING ORGANIZATIONAL STRUCTURES

Because Christian congregations possess a sociological dimension that is *de jure humano* (by human design), they have liberty to organize themselves in ways that they determine are most beneficial to God's mission (Romans 14:1–12; Galatians 5:13–14; Colossians 2:1). This is why there is such a diversity of organizational models and social structures among Christian congregations. In the sociological dimension, congregations will organize themselves differently because they exist in different sociological contexts and conditions.

Accordingly, there is latitude in how churches are organized. Some congregations will be more hierarchical in structure, while others will reflect a flattened structure. Some will utilize a church council, while others will employ a board of directors. Some churches will organize around staff, while others will be exclusively volunteer led. There is no exclusive organizational model that God has prescribed for local congregations as long as they respect His design for pastoral leadership as well as the priesthood of all believers. There is liberty and latitude in the sociological dimension to experiment with varying options to see what works best. We apply the ministerial use of reason and sanctified common sense, along with prayerful and biblical discernment, in order to decide how to organize a church.

Church leaders should not assume that there is a dominically prescribed structure of organization for their parish. Jesus mandated no congregational structure when He instituted the Church. The Book of Acts and the New Testament epistles provide scant information about how the early Christian congregations organized themselves, and what is there is mostly descriptive and not prescriptive. As a result, churches have latitude in the design of their organization.

Any organizational structure should be in accord with theological principles that are clearly taught in the Bible. In other words, it is not as if "anything goes" when designing a governance structure for a congregation. For example, the structure must uphold the divinely instituted pastoral office and its position of authority in the Church. It must promote the involvement of laypeople as affirmed by the doctrine of the priesthood of the baptized. The exercise of the Keys of God's kingdom should be appropriately assigned in the operations of ministry and mission. The latitude that a church has in organizing itself is still bound by doctrinal matters such as these.

It is true that various ecclesial traditions affirm historic approaches to organizing congregations and the practice of church polity. These are to be respected in Christian humility and harmony. Nevertheless, many traditions allow congregations to choose for themselves whether to establish church offices such as that of president, executive director, and board chairpersons. They can elect whether to have boards, councils, or working teams. They may organize their governance to include a church council or a board of directors. They may decide to make all the official decisions via the congregational assembly or delegate those decisions to a leadership team. The form of government may be centralized or decentralized. Congregations have freedom to determine which form is best for them given their contexts and corporate priorities as long as they conform to the guidelines of their ecclesial traditions.

What is needed, however, is *some* form of structure that serves the needs and purposes of that congregation. The apostle Paul maintained that in the Church "all things should be done decently and in order" (1 Corinthians 14:33, 40; 2 Corinthians 8:20–21; Colossians 2:5). This includes the need to organize and administer the programmatic affairs of the parish. What follows in the next chapters is a presentation of options in use by many churches so that you, as a leader in your congregation, may make an informed decision about which organizational design will best facilitate the advancement of mission and ministry in your distinctive context.

SUMMARY

Organizing the members of a local church is necessary because there is a sociological dimension to the Church. This dynamic involves coordinating lay leaders and volunteers in processes and programs to accomplish the goals of the spiritual dimension—the Church's Gospel ministry and mission. This organizational expression is oftentimes embodied in structures such as boards, councils, and committees.

Congregations have freedom to construct these structures in ways that best fit their distinctive culture and context, as long as they advance the Church's mission and do not violate biblical teachings.

CHAPTER 3

CONGREGATIONAL ORGANIZATION **EXEMPLIFIED**

Walther's Proper Form of a Lutheran Congregation

Guidance on practicing congregational organization in a theologically faithful manner is found in a document written over a century and a half ago. Its author is Dr. C. F. W. Walther, and it was originally published in 1864. Its title, *The Proper Form of an Evangelical Lutheran Local Congregation Independent of the State*, alludes to its attention to congregational form and structure. In the book's foreword, Walther states that its content "represents a church *organization* as it has already been constituted here for 24 years."[25] Therefore, it provides helpful insights appropriate to the subject of this book—congregational organization.

As stated earlier, organizational structures in congregations vary depending on the context. Of course, the context of Pastor Walther's congregations in the middle of the nineteenth century differs significantly from what we observe today in the twenty-first century. Yet the principles by which Walther describes the organization of a faithful and fruitful Lutheran congregation are timeless and instructive.

25 C. F. W. Walther, *The Proper Form of an Evangelical Lutheran Local Congregation Independent of the State*, in *Walther on the Church: Selected Writings of C. F. W. Walther*, transl. John M. Drickamer (St. Louis: Concordia Publishing House, 1981), 124, emphasis mine.

They provide helpful direction to us today as we consider the options and opportunities for congregational organization.

Walther divides his work into three chapters. The first chapter focuses on the rights of a local congregation. The second chapter reflects on the duties of the individual parish. Chapter three, which contains 75 percent of the work, addresses the exercise of these rights and duties in practical ways. In each section, Walther richly supports his theses with quotations and references from Scripture, demonstrating that his conclusions derive from the authoritative Word of God.

It is clear that Walther prioritizes the spiritual dimension of the Church over the sociological one in that the first two chapters lay out the theology and purposes of the Church according to the Word of God. Chapter 1 concerns the rights of a local congregation and locates these rights in the Keys of God's kingdom. Walther writes: "All the rights of an Evangelical Lutheran local congregation are embraced in the keys of the kingdom of heaven, which the Lord gave to his whole church originally and immediately and in such a way that they belong to every congregation in equal measure, the smallest as well as the largest."[26] Walther locates the authority of a local congregation in these Keys and admonishes such a congregation "to do all things necessary for its administration."[27] He identifies the true members of the Church as "the believing Christians in it, [who] are called priests and kings before God, or the holy priesthood."[28] He goes on to identify the Church as the Bride and Body of Christ. Furthermore, Walther identifies the pastor of the congregation as its steward and servant.[29] It is obvious that Walther has in view here the spiritual dimension of the Church. He locates the congregation's authority in the Keys of God's kingdom, the power to forgive sins in the stead of Christ, carried out publicly by the pastor.

The second chapter then focuses on the duties of the local congregation. Having been given the Keys of the kingdom, what is the Church to do? It is noteworthy that Walther uses the term *duty* in this section.

---

26 Walther, *Form of a Lutheran Congregation*, 126.

27 Walther, *Form of a Lutheran Congregation*, 126.

28 Walther, *Form of a Lutheran Congregation*, 126.

29 Walther, *Form of a Lutheran Congregation*, 127.

This is a word that is infrequently used in contemporary society but has significant meaning and value. It brings to mind the Table of Duties in Luther's Small Catechism, in which Luther identifies the responsibilities assigned by God to Christians in their various callings in life.[30] Here Walther identifies the responsibilities God has assigned to churches. These duties direct the local congregation to action. These duties encompass the ministry and mission of the Church. According to Walther, the congregation is to see to it that

1. the Word of God dwells richly and has free course in its midst;
2. purity of doctrine and life is preserved in its midst and church discipline is exercised in regard to both;
3. all members are well cared for in bodily needs and don't suffer want;
4. all things are done decently and in order before God and before men;
5. the local congregation is devoted to the unity of the Spirit with the orthodox Church beyond its area in the bond of love and peace;
6. the whole Church is built up and promoted.[31]

In this second chapter, Walther articulates more specifically how the local congregation is to administer the Keys of God's kingdom the Lord has entrusted to it. He identifies the priorities to which the Church devotes itself in the spiritual dimension. The scriptural passages he quotes after each duty indicate more fully what that duty entails, in addition to demonstrating the biblical basis for each. For example, in the first duty, that the congregation should see to it that "the Word of God dwells richly and has free course in its midst," Walther quotes Colossians 3:16. This verse identifies the tasks of teaching, admonishing, and singing psalms and hymns as manifestations of how the Word of God dwells richly among us. Accordingly, the local congregation will attend to Christian education (teaching), proclamation (admonishing), and worship (singing) as means to achieve the duty.

30 SC "Table of Duties," *Concordia: The Lutheran Confessions*, 34

31 Walther, *Form of a Lutheran Congregation*, 128–131.

PUTTING THE PRIORITIES INTO PRACTICE

The practical implementation of fundamental duties of the Church becomes more explicit in chapter 3, entitled "Concerning the Exercise of the Rights and Duties of an Evangelical Lutheran Local Congregation." The primary focus of this chapter is on the *exercise* of duties by the congregation, that is, *how* the congregation—in actual practice—carries out its responsibilities in both the spiritual and the sociological dimensions. At this point, organizational dynamics are fully engaged. Here are summaries of what Walther identifies as practices to accomplish each duty:

"To see to it that the Word of God dwells richly and prevails in its midst."[32] Walther states that this duty is exercised "especially by establishing and maintaining the public ministry of the Word in its midst."[33] This is accomplished first by calling a pastor. Walther lays out in detail the process for doing so, and it is clear that this requires significant organization of many participants: voting members, lay leaders, and other pastors for consultation. This duty obligates the congregation to organize weekly worship services and to administer the Sacraments of Baptism and the Lord's Supper. The baptized are to be instructed in the faith and publicly confirmed. The congregation extends pastoral care to those who are under trial, in sickness, or grieving. Weddings and funerals are conducted for members. Walther advocates that a congregation provide a parish school when possible.[34] These are the tasks and institutions that promote the ministry of the Word. The congregation is obliged to organize itself to execute such tasks and institutions in the intersection between the spiritual and sociological dimensions.

"To care for purity of doctrine and life and in both respects to discipline its members."[35] Walther maintains that this end involves the spiritual oversight of the pastor and lay leaders (elders) "in ruling,

32 Walther, *Form of a Lutheran Congregation*, 135.

33 Walther, *Form of a Lutheran Congregation*, 135.

34 Walther, *Form of a Lutheran Congregation*, 137–40.

35 Walther, *Form of a Lutheran Congregation*, 140.

disciplining, and keeping order in the congregation."[36] Pastoral and lay leadership are essential to this task. These leaders see to the doctrinal integrity of the instruction and rites sponsored by the congregation. They shepherd the members of the congregation, seeing that all members confess the true faith and live according to it. They exercise congregational discipline when necessary and assure that the congregation makes an orthodox confession.[37] The execution of these practices doesn't happen unintentionally. They require purposeful organization and administration, planning and programming. Although they are responsibilities carried out primarily in the spiritual dimension, they also have a sociological expression to which the pastor and lay leaders give due diligence.

"To care for its members also in earthly needs."[38] In fulfilling this duty, the Christian congregation demonstrates the virtues of mercy and compassion, which are fruit of the Spirit's work in its midst. But clearly, these earthly needs fall into the realm of the First Article since they deal with physical needs of members. In Walther's view, the first task is to care for the called workers and their families (pastors and teachers) in their bodily needs so that they are not distracted from the spiritual responsibilities of their callings. Similarly, the congregation is to extend charitable beneficence to the poor, sick, and destitute among them and to those who suffer calamity and distress.[39] The effort to provide these earthly supplies to the needy requires organization. It requires the gathering and distribution of resources. The sociological dimension of the Church must be mobilized in order to accomplish her spiritual responsibilities.

"To see to it that all things in it are done decently and in order."[40] In this section, more than in the others, Walther addresses the organizational aspects of congregational life. He directs congregational leaders to give due diligence to administrative matters such as the conducting of meetings, record keeping, document management, financial accounting, and facility maintenance. Walther prescribes

36 Walther, *Form of a Lutheran Congregation*, 141.

37 Walther, *Form of a Lutheran Congregation*, 141–45.

38 Walther, *Form of a Lutheran Congregation*, 145.

39 Walther, *Form of a Lutheran Congregation*, 145–47.

40 Walther, *Form of a Lutheran Congregation*, 147.

the codification of a church constitution and written job descriptions for congregational officers.[41] Significantly, Walther claims that the congregation conducts this business "not only before the Lord but also before men."[42] Thus he expressly states that the congregation operates both in the spiritual dimension ("before the Lord," *coram deo*) and in the sociological dimension ("before men," *coram hominibus*). This section of Walther's work focuses primarily on matters of the sociological expression of the Church—officers, meetings, regulations, documents, procedures, policies, even organizational structure. Therefore, it is clear that he recognizes the need to attend to the administrative tasks that serve the advancement of the spiritual priorities of ministry.

"To seek the unity of the Spirit, in the bond of love and peace, also with the orthodox Church outside itself."[43] Here Walther addresses the need for trans-congregational relationships and unity. The local congregation is not to be an insular entity, disconnected from the broader Church. Instead, it should collaborate with other orthodox congregations to advance God's mission. This is done by praying for others, sharing a common confession of the faith, transferring members to sister congregations, receiving into membership those sent from them, seeking wise counsel from other churches, and giving aid to them in their need.[44] This goal clearly engages an ecclesiology that views the Church as the *unam sanctum*, and thus is soundly situated in the spiritual dimension. Yet for such trans-congregational cooperation and collaboration to happen, it is necessary to organize. This is manifested today in organizational entities such as circuits, districts, synods, denominations, and even larger ecumenical endeavors.

"To do its share that the Church in general may be established and promoted."[45] This outcome is similar to the previous one in that it is concerned with the Church universal, what Walther calls the Church in general. It focuses especially on the missional duty of

41 Walther, *Form of a Lutheran Congregation*, 147–50. See Appendix 1 of this book, "The Congregation's Constitution and Bylaws," for guidance on developing the important documents of a church's constitution and bylaws.

42 Walther, *Form of a Lutheran Congregation*, 130.

43 Walther, *Form of a Lutheran Congregation*, 150.

44 Walther, *Form of a Lutheran Congregation*, 150–52.

45 Walther, *Form of a Lutheran Congregation*, 153.

the Church. Walther asserts that "a congregation should be zealous to spread the written Word of God," and it "should do its share that the Gospel may be brought to those sitting in darkness."[46] The local church undertakes this outreach effort in its own context but also partners with other congregations to train pastors and missionaries and send them to advance the mission of God throughout the world. This collaboration "serves and promotes the glory of God and the spread of His kingdom."[47] Organizational structures and practices will need to be implemented for the congregation to accomplish this missional outcome.

SEARCHING FOR STRUCTURE

For the most part in this work, *The Proper Form of an Evangelical Lutheran Local Congregation Independent of the State*, Walther identifies the congregational duties without going into detail about the administrative tasks needed to get the goals done. The reader may search for a prescribed organizational structure for a Christian congregation in Walther's writing, but such a search will be in vain.

Walther demonstrates great insight in recognizing that, whereas the congregation's prescribed duties are timeless and universal (i.e., expressing the spiritual dimension of the Church), the administration and execution of those duties in practice (i.e., the sociological manifestation) will vary from place to place. Walther originally presented this work as an essay for the Missouri Synod's Western District convention in 1862. At that time, the territory of the Western District was vast, extending from Illinois to California. The context for ministry in the western frontier was vastly different from that of the settled lands adjacent to the Mississippi River. Thus, to prescribe an organizational model as "one size fits all" for distinct congregations in differing contexts would be unhelpful. Even worse, such a mandate would violate Walther's theological understanding of the Church and his position

46 Walther, *Form of a Lutheran Congregation*, 153.

47 Walther, *Form of a Lutheran Congregation*, 154.

that congregations possess the inalienable liberty to choose their form of governance.[48]

Accordingly, a clearly defined organizational structure is not readily discernable in *The Proper Form of an Evangelical Lutheran Local Congregation Independent of the State.* At most, Walther describes some possible administrative officers and practices, but these are not made obligatory to congregations. They are a matter of *adiaphora*, and thus may vary from context to context. This recognizes that an organizational structure is *de jure humano*, of human design, not *de jure divine*, of divine mandate. Each congregation is to determine how best to accomplish its God-given duties in its own distinctive context of mission and ministry.

Having said this, however, there is one organizational entity that Walther prescribed for every Lutheran congregation. That is the congregational meeting, which today is commonly known as the voters meeting. Walther writes: "For the conscientious, salutary, and God-pleasing exercise of their rights and duties it is necessary for all independent local congregations to arrange regular orderly public meetings in which are discussed, resolved, and executed such actions as are necessary for its self-government."[49] This assertion follows from Walther's claim that the rights of a local congregation derive from its reception of the Keys of the kingdom of heaven. Accordingly, the congregation possesses "the power and authority to do all things that are necessary for its administration."[50] Since the congregation is composed of laypeople as well as the pastor, the decisions for carrying out the church's duties are made by the laity and clergy as they gather in a congregational meeting. The organizational models we will consider later all accept and assume that the final authority, under Christ, for decision-making in a congregation rests with the members who gather in a congregational meeting. Yet even here, Walther does not dictate how often congregational meetings should be convened or precisely how they should be conducted. He simply states that meetings should

48 C. F. W. Walther, First Presidential Address, transl. Paul F. Koehneke, in *Congregation-Synod-Church: Basic Theological Principles Underlying LCMS Structure and Governance* (Concordia Historical Institute Quarterly, Volume 23 Edition 1, April 1960 , pp. 12-20), 43.

49 Walther, *Form of a Lutheran Congregation*, 132.

50 Walther, *Form of a Lutheran Congregation*, 126.

be "regular" and "orderly."[51] Thus, local churches may schedule their congregational meetings as often as they deem necessary and conduct them following an order that seems most fitting.

Walther also assumes that lay leaders will be engaged in the work of the Church. These he refers to as *officers*. He even names some of these, including congregational chairman (p. 149), secretary (p. 147), treasurer (p. 147), and custodian (p. 148). Groups of officers are also mentioned, including elders (p. 141), almoners (p. 146), and trustees (p. 148).[52] Again, these lay offices are mentioned by Walther in the spirit of "this is what I recommend" rather than "thus says the Lord."

Most significantly, Walther affirms the role of lay leaders in the administration of congregational affairs. Leadership in the Church is not the exclusive prerogative of the clergy. Regarding lay officers, Walther gives wise advice for administering their service. He writes: "All those (except the pastor) who administer an office in the congregation should receive written regulations drawn up by the congregation, in which their duties, together with their extent and limitations, are carefully defined. However, every member, if qualified, should be willing to accept such an office offered to him."[53]

Here Walther recommends that the responsibilities of each officer be clearly articulated (in writing) and their limitations be defined. This aligns with a practice that I will commend later, namely that each lay leader be soundly informed as to what his or her responsibilities are (termed as *ends*) as well as what the legal, ethical, and financial boundaries are within which they may undertake these responsibilities (labeled as *limitations*). Walther also encourages all qualified laypeople to serve willingly in congregational leadership positions. This is the spirit of willing volunteerism, which is affirmed as well in the book you are herewith reading.

---

51 Walther, *Form of a Lutheran Congregation*, 132.

52 It is significant that although Walther uses the title of elder and overseer for a group of lay leaders, he identifies their qualifications as those associated with deacons, quoting Acts 6:3 and 1 Timothy 3:8–12 (p. 141). He thereby distinguishes them from pastors who fill the divinely instituted Office of Public Ministry.

53 Walther, *Form of a Lutheran Congregation*, 149.

TAKEAWAYS FOR TODAY

Although the times and context of the congregations that Walther envisioned in *The Proper Form of an Evangelical Lutheran Local Congregation Independent of the State* differ significantly from those of today, many of the insights from this work can be applied to contemporary congregations. Especially relevant are principles about the intersection between the spiritual and sociological dimensions of the Church. Here are several conclusions derived from our analysis of Walther's essay.

First, Walther clearly affirms the need for organization in the local congregation. As he states, "The congregation must see to it that all things are done decently and in order, and this not only before the Lord but before men."[54] Each church must attend to organizing its activities in the sociological dimension (before men, *coram hominibus*) as well as in the spiritual dimension (before God, *coram deo*). This includes assigning roles to lay leaders (officers) and managing lay volunteers in the mission of the Church. Lay members as well as clergy participate in the congregation's governance.

Second, although both dimensions are engaged in the life of the Church, the sociological serves the spiritual. The plans and programs that humans execute (by human authority, *de jure humano*) play a ministerial role to the design and directives that God has for His Church (by divine authority, *de jure divino*). This is why Walther begins with "the keys of the kingdom of heaven, which the Lord gave to his whole Church originally and immediately,"[55] and he grounds all the duties and activities of the congregation upon this.

Third, the first initiative in organizing a church's activities is to identify its duties that advance the faithful administration of the Keys as prescribed by Scripture. Walther articulates six of these, which can be summarized as follows:

54 Walther, *Form of a Lutheran Congregation*, 130.

55 Walther, *Form of a Lutheran Congregation*, 126.

1. Education and worship (including the administration of the Sacraments)
2. Care for the members' spiritual welfare and sanctified lives
3. Care of the physical needs of the community
4. Attention to resources, especially of finances and property
5. Fellowship (both internal to the congregation and external in trans-congregational collaboration)
6. Outreach and mission

Once the God-given responsibilities are identified, then the humanly designed organizational structure can be formed around them and a strategy and tactics to accomplish them can be executed.

Fourth, the fact that Walther does not prescribe a set organizational structure for each and every congregation testifies to the flexibility and freedom that congregations have in this regard. Walther does affirm the place of the congregational meeting, which he sees as necessary for a congregation to exercise its rights and duties.[56] This is why congregations that are members of The Lutheran Church—Missouri Synod vest the authority for decision-making with the voters assembly. Yet this is a penultimate authority under the authority of God and His Word.[57] Walther is also careful to properly distinguish between the authority and responsibilities of the pastoral office and that of the laity.[58] But within the boundaries of these theological givens—the right of a congregation to govern itself and the proper exercise of the

56 "For the conscientious, salutary, and God-pleasing exercise of their rights and duties it is necessary for all independent local congregations to arrange regular orderly meetings in which are discussed, resolved, and executed such actions as are necessary for its self-government." Walther, *Form of a Lutheran Congregation,* 132.

57 "Matters of doctrine and of conscience are to be resolved unanimously according to God's Word and the confession of the church. . . . Adiaphora, however, that is, matters which in God's Word are neither commanded not forbidden, are to be decided according to the principles of love and fairness, after previous deliberation, in Christian order, by a majority of votes. . . . Should anything in the congregation be decided and established contrary to God's Word, such a decision and establishment is null and void and should be declared so and be rescinded." Walther, *Form of a Lutheran Congregation,* 134–35.

58 This is the first matter that Walther gives counsel on when he begins discussing the exercise of congregational duties: "The first step in the necessary care for the establishment and maintenance of the public ministry in a congregation is the election and calling of a pastor" (Walther, *Form of a Lutheran Congregation,* 136.) Walther then immediately identifies the responsibilities the pastor has toward the church as well as those which the church has toward the pastor.

pastoral office—the local church has freedom to organize itself with a structure and in a manner that it deems best.

In conclusion, Walther's *The Proper Form of an Evangelical Lutheran Local Congregation Independent of the State* provides insight and guidance for our efforts today to navigate the intersection of the spiritual and sociological dimensions of local church ministry. He makes the appropriate distinctions between these but also gives helpful counsel for executing them. The principles he espouses have application for today as we undertake to organize our congregations so that they might faithfully administer Christ's Keys and advance His kingdom.

SUMMARY

C. F. W. Walther provided guidance to congregations in the nineteenth century for organizing themselves in a faithful and effective manner. His principles have value for us as we navigate congregational ministry in the twenty-first century. Walther affirmed the need to organize, and he identified duties for congregations to organize around. First the God-given responsibilities are identified, then the humanly designed organizational structure, strategy, and tactics are developed in order to accomplish those responsibilities.

These responsibilities continue for congregations today. *How* this can be done in the contemporary context using various models of organizational structures is the concern of the next several chapters (Part 2) of this book.

PART II

OPTIONS FOR ORGANIZATION IN THE CHURCH

A variety of administrative structures are being employed by North American congregations today. Some are hierarchical, others are flattened. Some are staff-driven, others are lay-led. Some are complex, others are simple. Some are democratic in their form of governance; others are more representative in nature. Each of these models has distinctive strengths and weaknesses, and certainly some are more appropriate to a given context than others.

Nevertheless, there are basically three broad models of administrative structure that dominate the organizational landscape of Christian congregations in North America. These models fit into categories labelled as *working* boards, *managing* boards, and *governing* boards.[59] They regard the administrative board structure consisting of leaders, both professional and volunteer. The term *board* is used in this book to refer to the group of leaders in the congregation who are authorized (by employment, election, or appointment) to execute the programmatic priorities of the congregation and to oversee its organization.

The next three chapters present in detail the characteristics of each of these three broad categories. Chapter 4 will describe the *working board* model that has traditionally been used in Lutheran (and more generally, Protestant) congregations in North America. Chapter 5 analyzes the *managing board* model, which is similar to the traditional

59 James C. Galvin, "The Great Board Debate: How Should Ministry Boards Govern?" *Christian Management Report*, December 2003, 5–9. In this article, Galvin identifies five structural categories, but the final two (ratifying board and failing board) are corruptions of the original three categories and are not commended. Galvin's article is directed particularly to the overseeing boards of religious nonprofit and parachurch organizations, but the insights can be applied to local congregations as well. The ways in which I describe working and managing boards is similar, but not exactly congruent, with Galvin's descriptions. More recently, Galvin adds another category, the navigating board, which is utilized when there is an especial need to navigate change in the organization. See James C. Galvin, *Maximizing Board Effectiveness: A Practical Guide for Adaptive Governance* (Elgin, IL: Tenth Power Publishing, 2020), 39.

model but more streamlined. Chapter 6 will present the policy-based approach, increasingly being adopted by congregations with multiple staff members, the *governing board* model.

The nomenclature of working, managing, and governing boards is not universally familiar. Many pastors and lay leaders will be familiar with other terms that historically have been employed by their distinctive congregations or denominational traditions, such as church board, administrative council, leadership council, board of directors, leadership team, vestry, deacon board, and trustees. There is no uniform use of these terms in ecclesial parlance. For example, what one church calls its board of directors may look very similar to what another parish calls its vestry. Or one congregation's administrative council may equate to another's trustees.

The task is to recognize the characteristics of these models and categorize each church according to the way it reflects the distinctive characteristics of a given model. The following three chapters will present the characteristics of each of the three models—working board, managing board, governing board—and will identify potential advantages and challenges of each. This will give you the opportunity to discern which model your church fits into so that you might maximize its advantages and minimize its disadvantages. Or it may inspire you to change the organizational structure of your congregation from one model to a different one to better achieve its goals.

Organizing your church is not optional. You will do so for better or for worse. The goal of the following three chapters is that you organize your church for the better. This will happen when your congregation engages the option that best fits its culture and context, its mission and ministry.

CHAPTER 4

THE WORKING BOARD

The Traditional Model of Church Organization

The first option for congregational organization is the *working board* model. This is a more traditional approach to organization in that during the last half of the twentieth century it was the dominant model for structuring Protestant congregations.[60] The track record reveals both success and frustrations resulting from the use of the model.

GETTING TO WORK

The working board model is so named because the members of a given board are expected to directly do the work that is the board's responsibility—that is, the board members are *working*. They are directly engaged in the operational functions of the ministry focus of the board.

For example, under this model the members of the youth board plan the activities for the young people of the congregation and also execute those activities. They teach the teenagers on Sunday morning

60 Church consultant Herb Miller identified this model as typical among congregations in the United States. See Herb Miller, *Church Effectiveness Nuggets, Volume 23: Fine-tuning the Organizational and Communication Engine* (N.p.: Herb Miller, 2009), 4. Miller maintained that this structure had its heyday in the latter half of the twentieth century but is less viable in the twenty-first century.

and coordinate the Wednesday-night gathering of young people. Youth board members serve as youth counselors who lead the occasional weekend retreat at a nearby camp. They sponsor and publicize the fund-raising events that the youth participate in. This board is actively involved in doing the work necessary to fulfill the youth ministry in the church. Its members are very "hands on" in terms of their involvement in the operations of the ministry.

A SIMPLE STRUCTURE FOR THE SMALL CONGREGATION

This model may have a very simple organizational design. A simple structure is typical of a small church or of a mission plant in its early stages. The lay leaders assume responsibility for doing the work that is necessary for the church's functioning. In a small church, this structure is frequently incarnated in the regular (monthly, bi-monthly, or quarterly) congregational assembly meeting. Practically speaking, the small church uses these assembly meetings to administer the affairs of the church without the use of any other council or board (with the possible addition of an elders board to govern spiritual matters and a board of trustees to oversee property maintenance). The few elected officers of the congregation—president, secretary, treasurer—lead the meeting. The congregational assembly meeting is open to all voting members, who thereupon participate directly in much of the business of the church. This business includes both strategic decisions (such as approving a mission initiative) and operational matters (such as purchasing a new copy machine).

Usually in these small parishes, there is only one paid staff worker—the pastor. He preaches, leads worship, and provides pastoral care to members. He catechizes the young and an occasional new adult prospective member. He visits the sick and the homebound. But the other programmatic work of the church is done by lay volunteers. This work can include teaching Sunday school, serving meals and refreshments at gatherings, maintaining the facilities, and coordinating an occasional special event such as a weekend Vacation Bible School or a fundraising fish fry.

The point is that during the congregational meeting decisions are made regarding what work will be done and who will do it. It is expected that people who attend the meeting will volunteer to do the work, comporting with the officers who were elected for a particular responsibility (e.g., several volunteers sign up to paint the exterior trim of the building under the guidance of the head trustee). This is a manifestation of a working board because everyone who participates in the congregational meeting contributes to the necessary work. Each voter is expected to volunteer for some aspect of the congregation's efforts, and this work is delegated and distributed at the congregational meeting. This dynamic comports with the working board model.[61]

A COMPLEX STRUCTURE FOR THE MEDIUM AND LARGE CHURCH

The aforementioned simple working board model will rarely be used in a midsize church (150–400 average worship attendance) and certainly not in a large congregation (400+ average worshipers). The reason is that the church has become too large and complex to be maintained effectively and efficiently by such an elementary structure. But the working model can evolve into a more complex structure that will operate fairly well in the midsize congregation (but typically not as well in a large church). This occurs when a multiplicity of boards is assigned the responsibility of different programmatic areas. An example of this is a church with seven boards for the following ministry areas: worship, education, children, youth, service, fellowship, and outreach. A board of elders might be added to this list. Each of these program boards have several elected board members as well as one chairperson. Each of these elected members is expected to participate in the work assigned to the board.

Typically, an overseeing body associated with this model is called the church council, administrative council, or parish planning council. Notice that the term consistently used here is *council*. The council is

61 In a white paper entitled *The Five Types of Governance in The Lutheran Church—Missouri Synod,* James Galvin identifies several ways in which governance through the voters assembly can be improved (Elgin, IL: Galvin & Associates, Inc.), 2–4.

the assembly of the directors or chairs of each program board. This model was promoted in the latter half of the twentieth century and continues to have influence today.[62]

Although significantly more complicated in design than the simple congregational assembly approach to organization, this structure for midsize and large churches retains its identity in the working board category because the members of each board are expected to do the work for their programmatic areas. For example, the members of the public relations board are expected to promote the ministry of the church through various local media. In this case, one member might submit articles to the newspaper, another might manage the congregation's website, another might edit the parish newsletter, another might produce signage for the church. Accordingly, the board members directly participate in the day-to-day operations of public relations. They are doing the work.

In this more complex manifestation of the working board model, a superstructure usually exists to connect the program boards. This superstructure is the administrative council. It is composed of the executive officers of the congregation—president, vice president, treasurer, secretary—as well as the chairs or directors of the various program boards. The primary purpose of the regular meetings of this administrative council is to coordinate the activities of the various program boards. The presence of the chairs of each program board provides a linking pin function to coordinate the efforts of each board. Board chairpersons deliver reports of their respective boards' plans and proposals so that any potential conflicts between boards can be avoided. This is also a time in which larger congregation-wide goals and strategies can be discussed and developed. However, frequently at these council meetings, the operational issues and more localized foci of the boards take precedent over strategic planning for the whole.

This kind of organizational chart for a working board model may look like this:[63]

62 Here are two examples of texts that promote this model: Guido A. Merkens, *Organized for Action: How to Build a Successful Parish and Its Program* (St. Louis: Concordia Publishing House, 1959); Donald Abdon, *Organizing Around the Great Commission* (Indianapolis: Parish Leadership Seminars, 1977).

63 Examples of how each organizational model might appear in graphic form are depicted as organizational charts in the remainder of this book. Information on the purpose, design, and

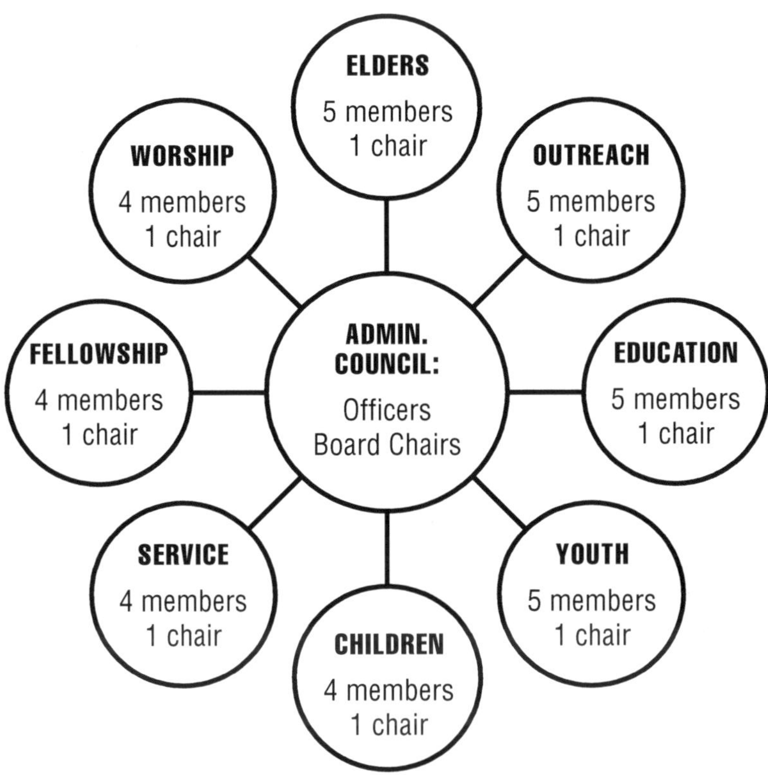

Many midsize congregations operate with this organizational structure. The structure is conducive to the programmatic orientation of the medium church, since the standing boards assure continued attention to their respective programs.[64] Some large churches also employ this structure, although it can become cumbersome in that context. Galvin observes that this model "is the best fit for congregations between 100 and 500 in weekly worship attendance. With less than 100 it's difficult to fill all of the ministry board positions. At more than 500, this form of governance begins to collapse under its own weight. A larger, more complex organization needs a more streamlined governance structure such as a board of directors."[65]

development of organizational charts is provided in Appendix Two, "Organizational Charts."

64 See the chapter on programs in David Peter, *Maximizing the Midsize Church: Effective Leadership for Fruitful Mission and Ministry* (Grand Rapids: Kregel Ministry, 2018), 69–85.

65 Galvin, *Five Types of Governance*, 7.

ADVANTAGES OF THE WORKING BOARD MODEL

There are several advantages of the working board model. The use of an administrative council and boards filled with willing workers has prevailed for decades in many American parishes because it is a relatively user-friendly approach to congregational organization. This model delivers benefits to many congregations; some are summarized as follows.

Just Do It

The first advantage of the working board approach is that it generally assures that the work in the program area will get done. Lay participants are elected to fill the program boards (e.g., education board, outreach board, youth board) because of their interest in the ministry focus of the board. As board members, they have a direct role in not only making decisions that impact the program area but also in participating in the work of that aspect of the congregation's ministry.

Ideally under this system the designated work gets accomplished, at least at a maintenance level. When it comes to the axiom "Just do it!" this approach to congregational organization gets the work done, albeit sometimes at a minimal level.

Easy Apprehension

A second advantage of the working board model is that it can be readily understood by participants. This approach is usually easy to operate in that board members intuit what work needs to be done, and they do that work directly.

Typically, when laypeople think of participating in the ministries of the church, they assume that they will be directly involved in the events and activities of a given program area. Frequently, the newly elected board members have already been informally involved in the program area, and so they have familiarity with its scope and nature. In addition, those who serve as board members do not necessarily need to be leaders. They only need to be workers. It is best that the board chairpersons are developed as leaders. But the three to five other members of each board need not be trained very extensively for their work. They are simply released to do the necessary work. Figuring out how to do the work isn't rocket science. Most lay volunteers can learn how to participate in a working board quite readily and easily.

Perpetuating Established Priorities

A third advantage of this model is that it brings continuity to the programmatic emphases of the parish. Because the program boards are *standing* boards, they will be perpetuated throughout the lifespan of the congregation (unless a board is dropped from the official structure, usually by a change in the bylaws).

In other words, since there is a Board of Christian Education, it can be assumed that work will be ongoing in educating young and old in the congregation. Since there is a Board of Parish Fellowship, one can expect that some form of fellowship promotion will continue in the congregation's community life. Thus, at any given time, church members can assume that the necessary work of the congregation is being done by the responsible program boards.

Promotion of Participation

A fourth advantage of this model is that it involves many people in the work of the parish. The assumption is that the more people participate, the better. A congregation that values lay member participation in the execution of its ministry will view a multiplicity of elected lay officers and board members as beneficial.

It is not uncommon that a congregation using this model will involve forty or more elected officers.[66] Their participation, it is assumed, helps them to be connected to the congregation and its ministry. It enables them to exercise the gifts for service that the Holy Spirit has entrusted to them. This high number of participants may be a distinctive benefit of using the working board model.

66 For example, if a church, following the typical pattern, has eight program boards, and there are five members on each board, this totals forty elected positions. Add to this the council leadership of the congregational president, vice president, secretary, and treasurer, and the total increases to forty-four elected participants in the working board structure.

CHALLENGES OF THE WORKING BOARD MODEL

There are also possible problems associated with the working board approach. These are not inherent to the model—that is, they do not of necessity *have* to arise because of its design. But experience shows that these problems frequently develop in the life of some congregations that employ a working board approach.

Neglect of a Unified Strategic Direction

The first potential pitfall is that the congregation's boards and council focus so much on the operational aspects of doing the work assigned that they neglect the strategic matters of the church. When board members are responsible for doing the work of their program areas, this operational work oftentimes consumes most of the available time and energy of the volunteer workers. The focus on executing the work of the program area impels an emphasis on operational details rather than the larger strategic picture.

The peril in this is that board members often become so consumed with the everyday and ongoing operational matters of the parish that they don't have time for the larger strategic perspective. They attend to the multitude of short-range matters of maintaining their programs, all to the neglect of long-range planning. They are so busy focusing on each operational step that needs to be taken that they fail to look up to the horizon and a grander destination. They get lost in the weeds and miss the larger vision of the congregation.

The neglect to do strategic visioning leads to a perpetuation of the status quo—doing the same operational tasks year after year. That's all that the volunteers who man the working board have time or energy for. This situation leads to the loss of positive change and of responsiveness to an ever-changing environment. It may contribute to the maintenance-only mode that typifies many congregations.

Mired in Meetings

A second potential disadvantage of the working board model may arise because of the multiplicity of board meetings that sometimes result. In this situation, much of the activity that gets done is merely that of gathering for meetings.

Board meetings typically involve ninety minutes or more of the participants' time. Add this to the obligation to do the base level work prescribed for the board, and many busy volunteers will have little time to be optimally productive. In the case of the board chairpersons, they also have the added responsibility of attending regular council meetings. It is not uncommon for additional ad hoc meetings to be called to address particular needs or issues.

As a result, a disproportionate amount of volunteers' time is devoted to participating in meetings. Energy is invested into attending meetings rather than in producing fruitful ministry. This is the pitfall manifested as "taking minutes and wasting hours" that was lamented in the earlier vignette.[67]

One way to reduce unproductive time spent in meetings is to require that *written* reports by board members be submitted several days before each meeting (by email or online social networks). This enables the other board members to read the reports and become familiar with them before the meeting, making discussion time during the meeting more productive. It also prevents board members from spending time unnecessarily on verbal ministry reports, which often are somewhat slipshod in both preparation and presentation. It is also possible for board members to meet online (virtual meeting), which reduces transportation time required when gathering in person.

Demand on Human Resources

A third potential peril with the working board model is that the structure can overextend beyond the human resources available to service it. Finding the manpower to fill thirty to fifty elected positions is a monumental task in a typical large church, let alone a midsize or small one.

67 Herb Miller reports that a majority of church members regard service on a church board to be unfulfilling unless the organizational structure accomplishes ministry impact rather than merely attending meetings. See Herb Miller, *Fine Tuning the Organizational and Communication Engine*, 4–5.

Pity the nominating committee that is given this responsibility! This oftentimes results in several positions on the board being left unfilled, meaning that the work assigned to those positions doesn't get done.

Another potential result is that less qualified candidates are recruited and elected to boards simply to meet the quota mandated by the bylaws. The nomination committee can be driven to the point of desperation so that it simply fills slots with warm bodies. The result may be that many participants are involved but the quality of the work becomes subpar.

WEIGHING THE VALUE OF THE WORKING BOARD OPTION

These are the pros and cons that must be considered when operating with a working board structure. The good news is that many of the potential pitfalls of this model can be avoided if handled correctly. The bad news is that many congregations that utilize this model continue to perpetuate some of the problems to which this structure is prone. Sometimes this approach can become so bureaucratic that it collapses under its own weight. If the working board model fails to mobilize a congregation to achieve its potential, then it may be time to consider another option for organizing the work of the laity.

CHAPTER 5

THE MANAGING BOARD

The Streamlined Model of Church Organization

The second major type of organizational structure available for use by congregations, broadly speaking, is that of the managing board. This model is so named because the members of the board are expected to *manage the work* that is designated as the board's responsibility but not to be directly active in the work. That is, the members of these boards do not do the work of ministry, but they see to it that it is done by others, while assisting those others when necessary.

HANDS OFF AND ON

The managing-board model is distinguished from that of the working board in the same way that supervising is distinguished from operating. When involved in operations, the elected members of the board personally perform the work that is assigned to the board; they *do* it. However, members of the managing board actively oversee the operations carried out by others; they *see* that it gets done. The difference is between *directly doing* (working board) and *directing the doing* (managing board). James Galvin defines the managing board as follows:

> Managing boards . . . have formal board meetings, hear reports and actively manage the organization. They make all the big decisions, set the budget, take responsibility for fund raising, and step in whenever problems arise. They like to keep their hands on the wheel. You can find managing boards in organizations of all sizes.[68]

This description can be applied to the coordinating lay council of a church, typically of a midsize congregation (150–400 average worship attendance) but sometimes of a small church or of a large one. The members of this council collaborate with the professional program staff, including the pastor. They actively manage the programmatic organization of the church by attending both to the strategic decision-making and to the operational matters of the programs. In managing the ministry of the congregation, the council members assume a hands-off/hands-on approach. That is, they delegate responsibilities to others but do not remain at a distance from those who are doing the work. Their hands are frequently involved in assisting in the operational work of their program areas. They "keep their hands on the wheel."

CONSTITUTING A MANAGING BOARD

The managing board in a church is typically manifested as the administrative council. It is composed of lay officers: the congregational president, vice president, secretary, and treasurer. It also involves the elected directors of the various program areas. But this is where the main difference exists between the managing and working board models.

As demonstrated in the previous chapter, in the working board design, each of the program areas are executed by a team of elected lay workers. There might be seven program boards, each responsible for a specific area of ministry, and each composed of five elected workers. These board members are responsible to do the work of the ministry assigned to the board, thus it is called a *working* board model.

68 Galvin, "The Great Board Debate," 7.

But in the managing board design, each program area is attended to by only one elected lay leader. This person is the director of the program area. Obviously that person cannot do all the work assigned to the program area. That would be beyond her limits of time and energy as a volunteer. But she is not expected to do it all, in fact she is prohibited from doing it all. She is not to do the work but to manage it. She is to see that it gets done by others. She is to appoint other lay workers and assign to them a task or role, guiding and directing them in their responsibilities as they have need. The program area director delegates the work to others and manages their efforts. For example, in the area of Christian Education, the director would recruit and train lay volunteers to be this year's Sunday School superintendent, and next year's Vacation Bible School director, and someone else to coordinate the small group program, and so on. Essentially the director manages others who do the work. An organizational chart of the managing board model would look something like this:[69]

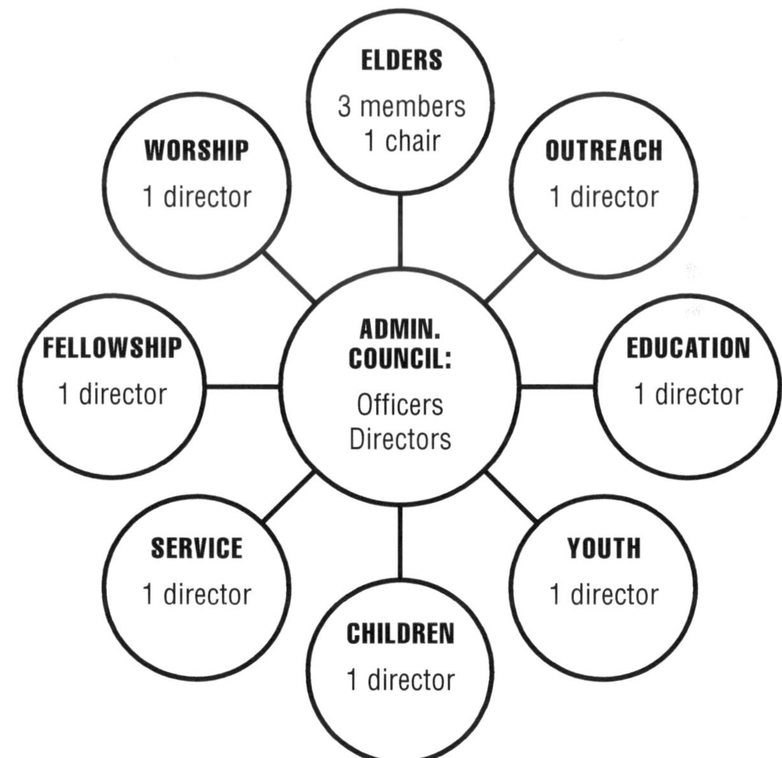

69 This graphic includes a Board of Elders, since some congregational polities will require such, and usually it is composed of more than two members.

Although this graphic depicts the basic structure of the managing board model, there are additional elements at play. First, a distinction can be made between ministry program areas and resource areas. The ministry program areas might include worship, education, outreach, and youth. These are areas in which ministry is carried out in the name of the congregation. The resource areas might include finances, property, and supplies. For example, a layperson might be elected to oversee the physical plant of the parish (property director). This is not a ministry focus itself, but it is needed to support the other programmatic areas of ministry. The finance resource director might be the elected lay treasurer, especially in smaller size operations. Ordinarily, both program area directors and resource directors would attend the regular meetings of the managing council.

INTEGRATING PROFESSIONAL STAFF

If the congregation employs paid program staff, these should interact directly with the elected lay directors for their respective areas of ministry responsibility. For example, the church's called assistant pastor overseeing education and youth would collaborate with the lay director of the education program area and the lay director of the youth program area. They together would lead these programs by managing others to do the work required. In the case of the youth program, the lay director would work with the assistant pastor to recruit adult counselors, teachers for the Sunday morning youth classes, and coordinators of fund-raising activities. The theory here is that professional staff and volunteer lay leaders work collegially to balance staff and lay participation. The challenge is that clear expectations and appropriate boundaries need to be established so that professional staff and lay directors can work in harmony.

Usually if a professional staff person is assigned to a program area, the burden of management is less heavy on the lay director. The expectation is that the staff worker will do most of the heavy lifting when it comes to managing the program. In some congregations using this arrangement, the elected lay program director essentially serves as a consultant to the staff worker, providing a voice from the lay perspective for the functioning of the program. In this context, the management of the congregation's ministry programs becomes staff driven, and the lay director plays a supportive role.

THE APPRENTICE

There is another important option available to the managing board model that may improve its functioning. This involves electing not only one lay director for each program area but also an assistant. This assistant would be given assignments from the director as necessary.

There are two advantages to this arrangement. The first is that the load of managerial responsibility is shared by two laypeople rather than being shouldered by only one person. The second is that the assistant receives on-the-job training so that he eventually becomes the director. In fact, this is the intended outcome—that the assistant is apprenticed to become the next director of a program area. The director and assistant would collaborate to delegate work to others and to manage and oversee their efforts.

Ordinarily under this arrangement, only the director attends the regular administrative council meetings. But occasionally the assistant could do so either with or instead of the director. This gives the apprentice an opportunity to observe the functioning of the council in preparation for his eventual elevation to it. The point is that leadership and management skills are taught to and caught by the assistant in the apprenticeship process, thereby equipping him to take the reins when the director's term of service is completed.

The more complex managing board model, which involves both an elected director and an elected assistant, might look like the schema on the next page:

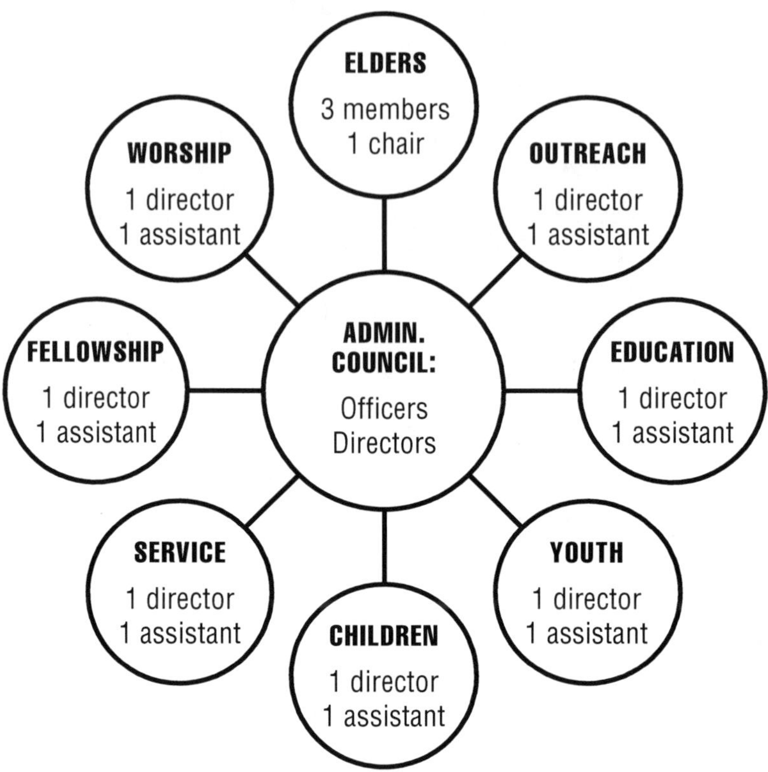

Since in this diagram there are seven program areas, and there are two lay volunteers serving in each ministry area, at the beginning of each term, fourteen laypeople would be on the slate for election. However, remember that the assumption is that the assistant from the previous term will continue as director in the new term. Accordingly, only seven new candidates would need to be recruited by the nominating committee each term.[70]

70 This graphic includes a Board of Elders with more members than a director and assistant, since some congregational polities will require such a board to be composed of more than two members.

ADVANTAGES OF THE MANAGING BOARD MODEL

Just as the working board model has potential advantages, so also the managing structure can bring rich benefits to the participation of lay members in ministry. What are those possible advantages?

Accommodation of Ad Hoc Involvement

The managing board model is conducive to the attitudes of many busy people today. It aligns well with their willingness to invest time and effort into a cause. A decreasing proportion of the North American population is willing to serve on formal boards and committees. They do not envision such participation as a valid use of their time. They wish to engage in ministry rather than meetings. They want to invest their volunteer time and energy in life-transformational causes rather than institutional committee gatherings.

The managing model accommodates this disposition in that most of the recruitment is for ad hoc involvement. Granted, the program area directors and elected officers must attend the regularly scheduled meetings of the administrative council, but this involves no more than a dozen people. Everyone else is recruited and appointed for a specific task that is usually short term. The ministry area directors select and appoint workers who evidence passion and initiative to tackle a specific mission or ministry effort.

Accordingly, most participants in the programmatic work that is done under this model are people who are given a task, equipped and resourced to do it, and managed along the way by the directors (and staff). They are released to serve a cause for which they are passionate and gifted, without having to be involved in many meetings and much administrative protocol. When the task is completed, they can celebrate their contribution to the accomplished goal. This mode of participation may greatly increase people's efficiency and effectiveness, resulting in a more gratifying experience.

Streamlined and Simple

A second advantage of this approach, compared to the more complex working board model, is that it is a simpler structure. There are far fewer elected positions, generally about 75 percent less than that which is required by the working board structure. Of course, these fewer positions must be filled with those who are truly able to manage, but this enables the search process for such leaders to be more focused and attainable.

Leadership Formation

The third positive outcome of this design is that it intentionally develops leaders. The directors of the program areas are entrusted with not only management but also leadership responsibilities. Granted, the tasks of recruiting and directing volunteer workers require management skills. But it also demands skills in leadership—as each program director develops a vision and strategic direction for her respective ministry area and aligns this with the congregation's mission. Her role of enlisting and motivating others to participate in this ministry area also manifests leadership skills.

If the design of this organizational structure includes the apprenticeship process that assigns an assistant to each program director, this is an ideal arrangement for forming new leaders. A process of leadership development that will be detailed in chapters 8 and 9 can be applied under these circumstances. The apprentice is immersed in the work of the ministry area and observes someone who models an appropriate role of leadership to imitate. When given assignments by the director, the apprentice can innovate new initiatives and gain skill in inspiring others to participate. This on-the-job training is an ideal context not only for management skills to be formed but also for the ability to lead.

A Strategic Voice

A fourth potential strength of this model is that it enables those who develop the strategic plan for the congregation to actively manage their areas of responsibility related to that plan. Or put inversely, those who manage the ministry (the program directors) are directly involved in its strategic design. This differs from the next model that will be presented, the governing model, in which those who design the strategic direction of the congregation (i.e., mission statement, vision, critical targets/priorities, etc.) are *not* the ones who manage and execute the strategy.

The advantage of the managing board system in this regard is that those who are responsible for administering ministry have a say in what that ministry should be. It is difficult to retain volunteers in leadership positions, and even in management roles, who do not have a voice in strategic decisions that impact their area of management. Program area directors in the managing board system have that voice and power.

Adaptability to a Staff-Run Church

A final advantage that this model may provide is that it can fit into a staff-driven structure. If the congregation has an adequate number of paid program staff, it is best that these professional workers be given primary responsibility for managing the program areas assigned to them. However, many congregations still value the principle that laypeople have an official voice and direct participation in the administration of the ministry programs.

To assign a staff person a working board of five or six elected officers is often inefficient and can lead to frustration, especially on the part of the staff worker. But the assignment of a single elected layworker to support and collaborate with the staff person can be both efficient and effective, as long as both have clear expectations about their respective roles. This system of partnering paid staff with elected volunteer leadership can promote the voice of the laity in a staff-led system.

CHALLENGES OF THE MANAGING BOARD MODEL

The significant benefits of the managing structure do not mean that it is devoid of potential difficulties. In this fallen creation, there is no perfect organizational system, just as there are no perfect people who participate in it. There is no utopian design of congregational governance! Possible pitfalls exist that are distinctive to the managing board model. This is not to say that these problems are inevitable, for each one can be overcome to some degree if done correctly. But experience indicates that the following problems can arise when a church implements this distinctive organizational structure.

Unqualified Lay Directors

The most obvious peril associated with this system is that incompetent lay volunteers are elected to manage ministry program areas. Since there is only one director of each program area, the effectiveness of that program will stand or fall on the competence—or lack of such—of the lay director. This is the Achilles' heel of the managing board model. It is possible in the working board model for fellow board members to pick up the slack when a colleague on the board is failing. But such a safety net does not exist in the managing board model, since there is only one director of each program area.

Even in an arrangement that utilizes an assistant director, it can hardly be expected that this apprentice will fill the leadership vacuum immediately and effectively. That is not his role, nor should it be expected of him. This issue is less critical in a situation where paid staff have primary responsibility for a program area. In this case, the staff person will see to it that the necessary management of the system occurs. But it also defeats the purpose of having a lay director to collaborate with.

Thus, the primary challenge in facilitating a managing board model is to supply competent lay volunteers to do the managing. This is easier said than done. First, there is a limited pool of people in the congregation who have potential to be effective managers. In order for them to find fulfillment in this role, they must enjoy managing others. Otherwise, they will experience frustration.

It is relatively easy to find volunteers to do operational work (such as is expected from the members of a working board). But typically, only a small proportion of a congregation's membership has the gifts and willingness to manage others. The challenge in the managing model is finding and forming willing volunteers from this diminished pool of candidates.

Finding the Time

Managing an entire program area of a congregation can demand much commitment and effort. Accordingly, many people do not have the time or energy to do this. It can be a demanding role to oversee a ministry such as education, youth, or outreach.

The management of an entire ministry area in many churches is time-consuming. This is a major reason so many parishes opt to fill such positions with paid staff who are employed to invest the necessary time and effort. Thus, it is a significant challenge to find qualified and competent candidates who have the time available to offer to this service.

Keeping Hands Off

Related to this challenge is the propensity of many program directors to move from managing the work of the ministry area to directly doing that work. The skills needed for management include recruiting others and delegating work to them. Sometimes directors find this to be so difficult that they decide it is easier to do the work themselves. But then they become a one-person (or if an assistant is used, a two-person) working board. And the work is too much for that arrangement! The result is that much of the work isn't done, or it isn't done well, or the program director becomes burned out, or all of the above.

Management Becomes Maintenance

Another significant challenge that can be endemic of the managing board model is that directors become so focused on the task of managing the program area that they fail to lead that area into new ventures. Their management efforts are limited to maintaining the status quo.

Typically, a distinction is made between the practice of management and leadership. Leaders take a long-range view, whereas managers embrace a more immediate perspective. Leaders have an eye on the horizon, while managers focus on present realities and resources. Leaders are more strategic in orientation, while managers are more tactical. Leaders are more innovative, challenging the status quo. Managers are more administrative, maintaining the established systems and protocols. Accordingly, management of ministry can devolve into mere maintenance of the ministry.

The qualities of management are essential to the managing board model—thus the ascription. However, leadership is also needed. Directors of program areas should always be looking for new and better ways to execute ministry and to advance God's mission. They should conceptualize outcomes by working from the future to the present. To do so, they need to envision the future and inspire others to pursue that vision. They need to budget their time to include strategic planning, not only tactical implementation. Otherwise, the ministry area will slip into the gear of maintenance and will increasingly lose relevance and impact.[71]

It is not uncommon for the lay directors to become so overwhelmed by the immediate challenges of management that they lack the energy and initiative to lead. They simply keep doing what's always been done. Once again, this is a less critical issue if professional staff are providing necessary leadership. But even in that circumstance, the ministry effort would be much enhanced by the infusion of supplemental lay leadership.

Disharmony

A final potential peril of the managing board model is the possibility for discord. This discord can be at several levels. The first level is between the lay program director and the other leaders in the congregation. In this system, much power is entrusted to the lay manager, at least for the area of ministry that he directs. It is possible that the manager becomes a maverick and leads the program in a direction that is contrary to the mission, values, and vision of the congregation. His management is out of alignment with the strategic direction toward which the other congregational leaders have covenanted. It is very difficult to pull the reins on this rogue leader, and the results can be messy and painful.

A second level of discord can arise between the director and the assistant, if that arrangement is used. There may be differences of values and vision. It may be a bad fit in terms of temperament and personalities. This is less problematic than the previously described level of conflict in that it is usually easier to intervene between the director and the assistant to bring resolution. Typically in such a case,

71 Chapter 9 offers guidance for forming lay leaders who are strategically-oriented and able to generate beneficial change.

the assistant will be asked to submit to the leadership of the director. If this fails to happen, the assistant may be dismissed. This is not a pleasant experience, but it usually doesn't have much adverse impact on the larger dynamics of congregational life. If resolution of the discord doesn't result and the duo is dissolved, it is still desired that the two parties be reconciled through a process of confession and forgiveness.

A third level of discord may arise in a context in which both a paid staff worker and an elected lay director share the responsibility to manage a program area of the church. This is the stickiest situation of the various opportunities for discord. The reason is because the congregation has entrusted authority to both parties, and both must be extended a high degree of respect and commitment. In this case, it is advisable that the senior pastor and/or congregational president step in to utilize a process leading to resolution and reconciliation.

Addressing the Perils

While the managing board model has much to be commended, it is not without the potential for problems. When considering implementing this model, one should be aware of these possibilities and seek to maximize the model's beneficial aspects and to minimize its pitfalls.

One key to overcoming many of these perils is to develop effective lay managers who will devote themselves to the tasks of recruiting, delegating, equipping, and supervising the work of others. A process will be presented in chapter 8 that can facilitate this outcome. Especially if the arrangement involves the apprenticeship dynamic, the competence of the assistant can be assessed before he assumes the director role. If it is apparent that he will not become adequately prepared for the responsibilities of managing a program area, then it is best to take the unpleasant step of finding a replacement for him partway through his term of service as the assistant. The hope then is that the new assistant will demonstrate the right stuff for the manager role by the time his apprenticeship is completed.

WEIGHING THE VALUE OF THE MANAGING BOARD OPTION

The working board model can become unwieldly in some medium- and large-size congregations, especially when forty or more lay volunteers are required to fill the board positions. Accordingly, many congregations opt for the managing board model that is more streamlined and less bureaucratic in design.

The managing board model has much to be commended for in its use in many congregations. Its design is simpler than the working board model, and its functioning can be more flexible. It is adaptable to contexts in which churches employ multiple professional staff workers, providing a collaborative balance between paid and lay leaders. This system is conducive to the use of ad hoc action teams that involve volunteers for short-term projects. It can provide a healthy context for the cultivation of lay leaders, especially through the use of an apprenticeship process. Program directors can experience significant satisfaction in determining the strategic direction of their ministry programs as well as in managing others to execute those programs.

But this model is dependent on qualified and competent lay leaders who fill the directorship positions. These directors must be able to manage others by recruiting, training, and equipping them as necessary. Although their efforts are hands-off in terms of operational efforts, they are to be hands-on in terms of organizing and managing others to do the work. Lay volunteers who have the capacity to fill such managerial roles are frequently hard to find. This is why it is critical for a congregation to offer a training process that develops the requisite management and leadership skills for these directors.

These are the realities to consider when operating with a managing board structure. If this structure fails in organizing a congregation to achieve its potential, then a third option may be preferred for structuring the efforts of the church's staff and lay workers. That option—the governing board model—is described in the next chapter.

CHAPTER 6

THE GOVERNING BOARD

The Corporate Model of Church Organization

The third basic model of organizational structure is one that is becoming increasingly popular in churches today. Most of the books recently published on congregational structure follow this model.[72] The model conforms to what James Galvin calls the *governing board* structure. Galvin describes this model:

> *Governing boards* hire an executive director or CEO and delegate to them responsibility. They make a sharp distinction between staff work and board work, and spend all their energies on board work. They use policies as a highly-leveraged tool to shape the organization and help move it forward. They try to stay away from operational decisions and don't micromanage

72 Some examples of recent publications that promote the use of policy-based governance in churches are Alan and Cheryl Klass, *Flexible, Missional Constitution/Bylaws* (Oak Park, IL: Mission Growth Publishing, 2000); Aubrey Malphurs, *Leading Leaders: Empowering Church Boards for Ministry Excellence* (Grand Rapids: Baker Books, 2005); John Kaiser, *Winning on Purpose: How to Organize Congregations to Succeed in Their Mission* (Nashville: Abingdon Press, 2006); Dan Hotchkiss, *Governance and Ministry: Rethinking Board Leadership* (Herndon, VA: The Alban Institute, 2009); Kurt Bickel and Les Stroh, *Structure Your Church for Mission* (Orlando: Strobicken Publishing, 2010); Ted Kober, *Built on the Rock: The Healthy Congregation (St. Louis: Concordia Publishing House, 2017).*

> the CEO. These boards follow the Carver model or are highly influenced by it.[73]

This description identifies the origin of this model of organization with John Carver, who laid out his design for board governance in his seminal book *Boards That Make a Difference: A New Design for Leadership in Nonprofit and Public Organizations.*[74] In this work, Carver presents a comprehensive theory with prescribed principles and practices for how the fiduciary boards of corporations and nonprofit organizations should operate. This model has been called policy-based governance because it affirms that the essential work of a board is to formulate policies that then are to be executed by a chief executive officer (CEO) working through his staff.

DISTINCTIVE CHARACTERISTICS OF A GOVERNING BOARD

The first thing to be noted about this model is that the elected board delegates responsibilities via policies to a CEO. Thus, when this model is applied to a Christian congregation, the assumption is that the pastor will function like a CEO. This may evoke a negative association among some Christians who envision a pastor acting as a powerful business executive, but this need not be the case. In many ways, the Carver model creates an arrangement in which the pastor is less authoritarian, not more so. This is because the pastor is expected to execute the will of the governing board that is composed of lay leaders who are elected by the voters assembly and charged to represent the best interests of the congregation.

Another assumption integral to this governance model is that the organization employs multiple paid staff members. It is for this reason that policy-based governance is becoming a dominant approach in large churches, which typically have numerous professional and paid staff. Multiple staff workers are also needed in midsize congregations, but the number of staff workers will be much fewer in the midsize

73 Galvin, "The Great Board Debate," 7.

74 Second ed. (San Francisco: Jossey-Bass, 1997).

parish as compared to the large one, so the utility of the Carver model is lessened.

A visual diagram of the governing board model, as it might appear in a typical large congregation—with a senior pastor and four paid professional program staff—might appear like this:

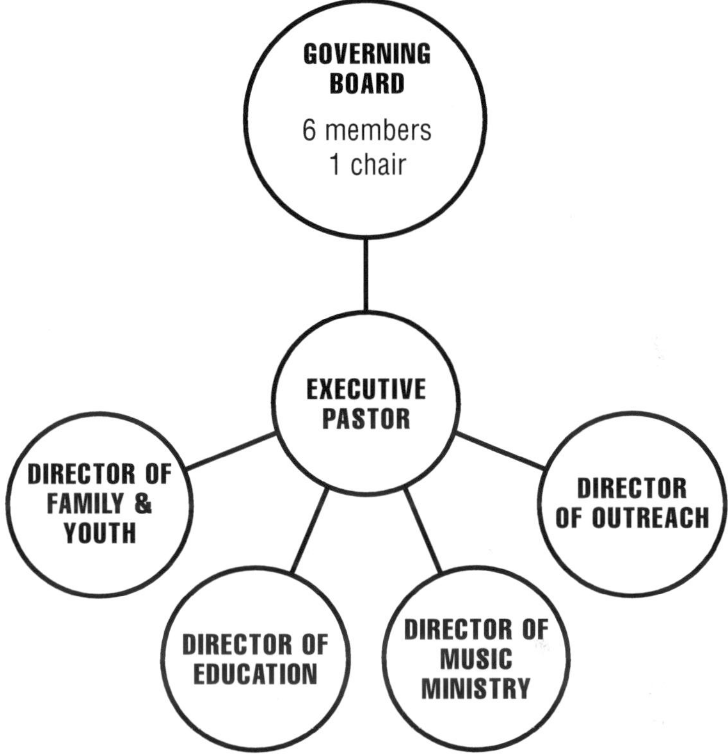

Note that the executive pastor is the linchpin for this structure. He is connected to the board of elected lay leaders by receiving its directives and being accountable to the congregation through this board. He is also connected to the employed staff, delegating the directives to them to execute in their respective areas of responsibility. The staff workers are accountable to the senior pastor and not directly to the board.

GOVERNING THROUGH POLICIES

In the governing board model, the primary role of the board is to govern. Board members are lay representatives elected by the congregational assembly who are responsible to make strategic and fiduciary decisions for the good of the congregation. Usually, the number of board members is a dozen or less and includes the congregational president as board chairman. The role of these board members—and this is important to note—is *not* to do the work of ministry nor even to manage it. It is to *govern* the ministry that is managed and executed by others, namely the pastor and staff.

The board governs by means of policies, and it is the board's primary responsibility to formulate these policies and to monitor how well they are being executed by the lead pastor and his staff. This is why the approach is commonly referred to as policy-based governance. In the original Carver model, there are four basic categories for the policies: organizational ends, executive limitations, board-CEO linkage, and governance process.[75]

Ends Policies

By far the most important of these categories is that of *organizational ends*. These are the policies that identify and articulate the mission of the congregation as well as the strategic goals and outcomes that will advance that mission. These are called *ends* policies because they express what the end results of the church's efforts should be. This fact demonstrates that the governing board should be focused on strategic matters—mission, vision, targets, goals, outcomes, and the like—and not on tactical or operational issues.

In this way, the board determines the missional direction of the parish as well as the concrete outcomes that are the result of the congregation's efforts. For example, the parish's vision may be to extend God's mission both locally and internationally. Congruent with this, an ends policy would state, "Mount Zion Church will each year sponsor and support at least three short-term mission trips beyond the borders

75 Carver, *Boards That Make a Difference*, 30–35.

of the United States." This is a concrete outcome that can reasonably be assessed as either accomplished or not.

Limitations Policies

The second set of policies are categorized as *executive limitations.* These serve to set limits on *how* the ends policies may be achieved. Such limitation policies form the boundaries within which those who execute the goals may operate. These usually identify legal and ethical restraints as well as limits for resources. They conscribe the methodology and behavior that will be used to pursue the ends.

For example, a limitations policy attached to the ends policy about international mission trips could limit the destinations to countries that are declared as safe by the U.S. State Department. It could also prescribe that the church will financially subsidize no more than 50 percent of the expenses for the trip (the remainder must be raised by the participants). It could also proscribe the participants from providing direct monetary contributions to the people being visited, meaning that the mission teams may contribute only labor and resources, not money, to those being served.

The formulation and delegation of ends and limitations policies will always be a very dynamic process. The board will continually assess the merits of these and will make revisions and adjustments to them as is necessary. These are the primary tasks of the governing board—to write new policies that are needed, to revise existing policies that are deficient, and to remove old policies that are no longer necessary.

Linkage and Process Policies

The other two categories of policies are much more static and less time-consuming for the board. The *board-CEO linkage* policies simply define how the board and the head pastor will relate to each other. The *governance process* policies identify how the board will function internally. These policies are established early on and remain relatively constant throughout the life of the board, although occasionally changes will be necessary. This is why the bulk of the time spent by the governing board will be devoted to policies related to ends and limitations. This includes not only formulating and revising them but also receiving reports about their execution.

EXECUTING THE POLICIES

The governing board creates policies, but it *does not execute* them. That is the responsibility of the head pastor, who functions as the chief *executive* officer (CEO). The ends and limitations policies are delegated to the pastor who is responsible to see that they are carried out. This pastor will attend the meetings of the board and will give input regarding the policies.[76] He will also report back to the board about how the policies have been executed. This is how the board holds him accountable. So, for example, the pastor at Mount Zion Church might report that in a given twelve-month period three mission teams were sent to international sites and that each of these were comported in a way that conforms to the limitations policies. The board would then commend him for conforming to the limitations directives.

In some churches, especially large ones, the CEO is not the lead pastor but another administrative executive who is on the staff. In such a situation, the senior pastor focuses primarily on preaching and worship leadership, as well as fund-raising and embodying the face of the organization. But typically only large churches have the finances or human resources to follow this option. Accordingly, in most parishes, the CEO is the lead pastor.

Once the lead pastor (or administrative executive) receives the policies that have been delegated to him by the governing board, he in turn delegates them to his staff. The staff members are then expected to implement the ends policies within the boundaries of the limitations policies. They do this by involving other laypeople in the projects and programs that advance these policies. Frequently these ad hoc groups of recruited laypeople are called ministry action teams.[77] In this role, the staff persons act as managers of the initiatives. They have freedom to devise the implementation of the ministry efforts as they please, if

76 In some congregations, the pastor sits on the board as one who has equal authority as the other board members. In a few churches, the pastor presides over the board and exercises more authority than the other members, somewhat as a *primus inter pares* (first among equals). This varies, depending on congregational and denominational polity. However, the original Carver model recommends that the CEO position be distinct from the board, as one who serves the board but is not a member of it (see Carver, *Boards That Make a Difference*, 104–105, 115–19).

77 The design and development of such ministry action teams is the subject of chapter 7.

it accomplishes the ends policies and is within the boundaries of the limitations policies.

The following graphic illustrates this in the case of the policies regarding three international mission trips. The lead pastor delegates the ends and limitations policies to the staff person who oversees missions, the director of outreach. This staff worker in turn recruits lay participants for the three mission teams, equips them for their task, and sends them forth, exercising innovation and creativity within the bounds of the policies. The line of downward delegation can be depicted by the arrows in this diagram:

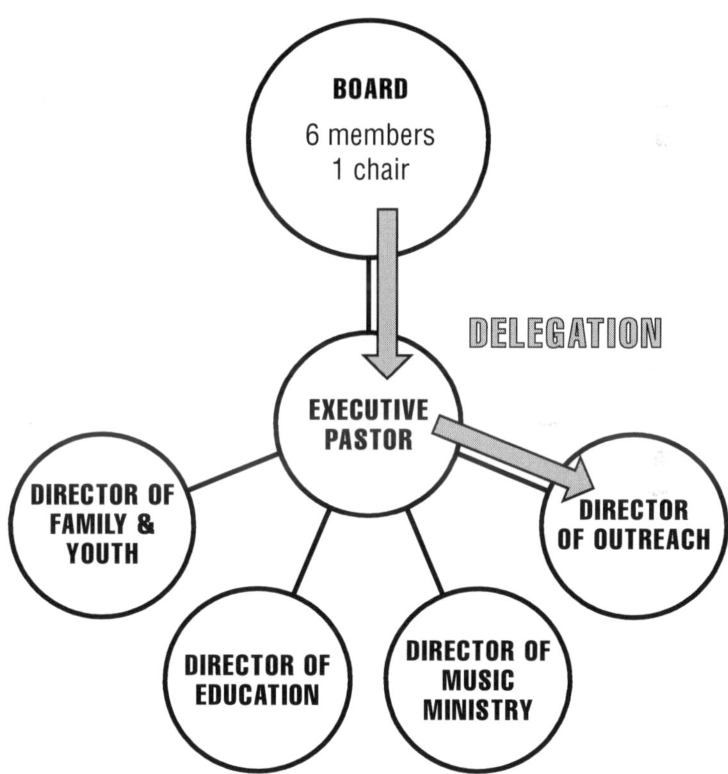

After the mission trips are completed, the director of outreach reports the outcomes of these efforts to the lead pastor, who in turn presents them to the board. Accordingly, the line of reporting goes upward from staff worker to lead pastor to the board of directors, as depicted in this diagram:

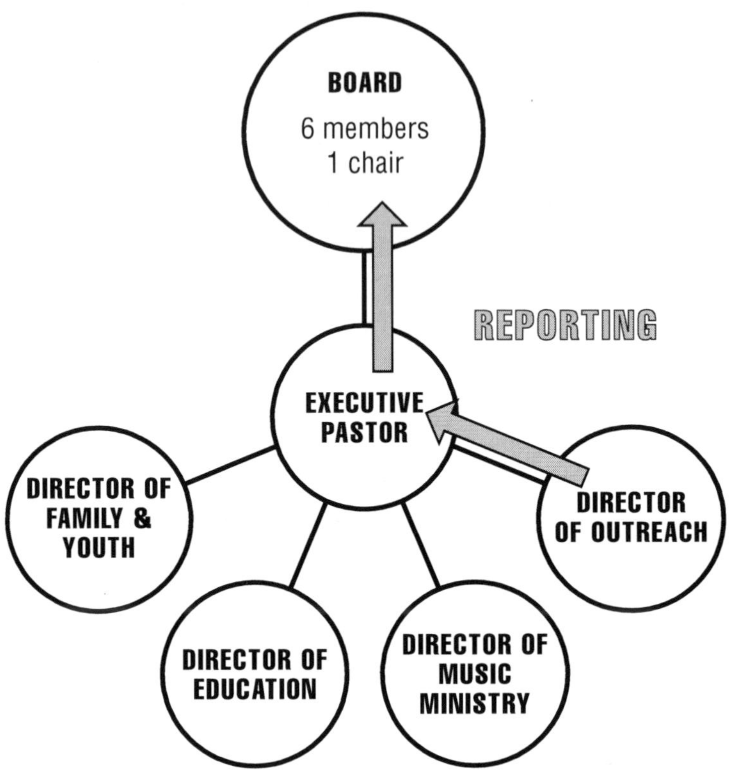

The lines of accountability are clearly established in this model as assignments are delegated downward by the board to the staff and reports move upward from the staff to the board.

In this model, professional staff workers do not determine the ends and limitations policies that impact their program areas, although they might influence these. In the pure Carver model, staff workers do not attend the board meetings. Oftentimes in congregational contexts, the board will request the input of the staff for strategic decisions. The board may ask staff workers to recommend or comment on policies that impact the ministries they oversee, even before those policies are formally adopted.

But ordinarily, a demarcation is set between the role of the staff and the role of the board. The board establishes the strategic direction for all the programs of the congregation. The staff attends to the tactical and operational matters of executing those strategic policies. Accordingly, there is a clear distinction between governance, which is the board's responsibility, and execution/management, which is the responsibility of the pastor and staff.

ADVANTAGES OF THE GOVERNING BOARD MODEL

The fact that many congregations throughout the United States and Canada are adopting the governing board model indicates that it has some advantages. It can be a structure that facilitates a congregation's efforts to be fruitful in ministry, effective in mission, and efficient in the use of its resources.

Clear Lines of Accountability

Perhaps the greatest strength of policy-based governance is that it provides a logical system for delegation of work and the reporting of results. In other words, it facilitates clear lines of authority and accountability. The lines of delegation and accountability in the governing board structure are depicted in this diagram:[78]

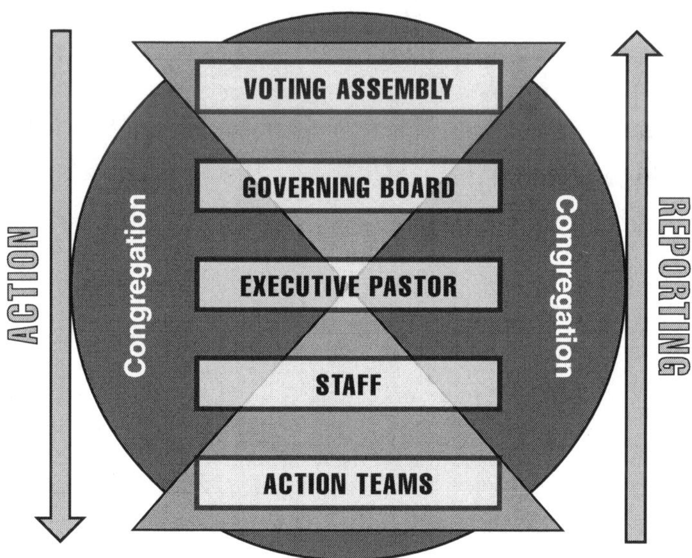

78 This diagram is based on one provided by a doctoral student whom I advised. See Matthew Bean, "The Relationship between the Board of Directors Governance Model and the Practice of Discipleship," (D.Min. diss., Concordia Seminary, 2008), 4.

The graphic displays that in this governance structure the highest authority (under God) in the congregation is the voting assembly, which in turn expresses the will of the congregational membership. This assembly elects a few (usually five to twelve) lay members to act as its representatives on the governing board. The governing board identifies and articulates the mission, strategic goals, and results that the congregation strives to achieve, as well as the legal, ethical, prudential, and financial boundaries for carrying out these outcomes. These are codified as ends and limitations policies and passed to the executive pastor to execute them. This pastor, in turn, delegates these to the paid staff workers, as is appropriate for their areas of responsibility. The staff personnel organize volunteers (congregational lay members and other interested participants) as action teams to accomplish the directives that accord with the ends and limitations policies. The results are then reported to the staff worker, who in turn reports them to the lead pastor, who reports them to the board. Finally, the board will provide a summary report, usually annually, to the voting assembly.

This system provides a clear process for delegating action (downward arrow) and for reporting results (upward arrow), and it holds the employed pastor and staff accountable. Professional staff workers must give an account to the executive pastor about the assignments given to them. And the pastor must give an account to the board about the completion of the policies that had been entrusted to him. It is not uncommon in other parish systems for accountability of professional staff to be elusive. This system provides a clear methodology for holding employed church workers accountable. Acting on behalf of the congregation, the board can demand performance from the church's employees and monitor delivery of that performance.

Clear Roles and Responsibilities

A second distinctive benefit of the governing board model is that it provides for a clear understanding of roles. Each component of the structure has clearly defined responsibilities. The board articulates the strategic direction of the congregation by formulating ends and limitations policies. If done correctly, this will keep the board focused on pursuing the mission, vision, and strategic priorities of the congregation without getting bogged down in the weeds of operational matters.

The executive pastor has the responsibility as CEO to execute these policies and see to the accomplishment of the strategic plan. As such, he exercises an executive leadership role. The program staff members are responsible for implementing the policies, and in this role, they exercise management functions. The respective roles are clear: the board governs, the pastor leads, the professional staff manages, and the members do the work. It is clear what all parties are responsible for.

Separation of Governance from Operations

Related to this is a third benefit that the board governance model can provide, namely, the clean separation of governance from management. The board governs and the staff manages. This provides efficiency through clear differentiation of roles. Just as a hospital board member doesn't perform surgery but sees to it that a technically trained surgeon does, so also a church board member doesn't directly execute or manage the parish's ministry. Instead, she makes it possible for the paid staff workers, who possess the appropriate expertise, to manage ministry in a strategic and ethical manner.

Allowing the professional ministry staff (full- and part-time) to actually manage the ministry of the church makes sense, rather than having lay boards do so. Staff workers are the ones trained and equipped to carry out ministry. They have the skill and competence for advancing the mission. In other systems, the board frequently becomes too involved in micromanaging staff or involved in operational matters. This model helps boards to remain focused on strategic, prudential, ethical, and fiduciary concerns.

Coordinated Design

A fourth benefit that can derive from the working board model is that it facilitates coordination of staff activities and oversight. The one who oversees the staff is the executive pastor, and only him. The one to whom staff workers report is the executive pastor, and only him. There are not multiple channels for gaining permission, nor multiple lines of reporting for accountability. This process streamlines staff-functioning significantly.

Freedom within Boundaries

A fifth advantage of this model is that it frees participants to do ministry. Some might perceive that the idea of being handed policies from a governing board is restrictive but usually the opposite is the case.

First of all, this arrangement can be freeing for the senior pastor. His administrative role is narrowed almost exclusively to the paid program staff. He delegates tasks and projects (aligned with ends and limitations policies) to employed staff workers and not to lay volunteers. The latter are much more difficult to hold accountable than the staff. Thus, the pastor doesn't need to invest an inordinate amount of energy with people who may not be dependable. If staff fail to be dependable, they can be held accountable for their failure, and reasonable consequences can be administered. Adapted for congregational use, the Carver model provides a senior pastor with a clear and logical system for supervising the programmatic activities in his church.

This system also frees staff workers to function creatively and without hesitation. They are liberated to manage their own ministry areas—within the bounds of the assigned policies—without having to wait for a program board or a program director to give them permission to act. In reality, there are fewer layers of authority required for a staff worker to gain permission to act. The board governance model reduces the opportunity for laypeople to micromanage staff, which can be a problem with the working board and managing board models.

Lastly, even volunteer lay workers may experience a greater degree of freedom. The bureaucracy that can develop around multiple program boards is replaced with an ad-hocracy as individual lay volunteers participate in ministry teams that actually do ministry rather than investing time in board meetings. These lay workers are recruited by staff professionals to serve on specific projects based on their interests and gifts. They participate in ministry teams for clearly defined initiatives with outcomes that bring fulfillment.

CHALLENGES OF THE GOVERNING BOARD MODEL

The use of policy-based governance in churches is becoming more commonplace. There are many good reasons for this, as is demonstrated by the advantages just identified. However, as more and more congregations have adopted the governing board model, several reoccurring problems have emerged. These pitfalls are not unavoidable or insurmountable, but any congregation that considers transitioning into this model should be aware of them and should work proactively to avoid them. These problems are more acute in small and midsize congregations than in large ones. Indeed, policy-based governance may not be the best organizational structure for most small and midsize churches.

The Need for Paid Staff

The foremost issue to recognize is that the application of the Carver model to a nonprofit organization like a church works best if that organization employs multiple paid staff persons. The model assumes that paid professional and semi-professional (i.e., part-time) staff workers will be responsible for the execution and management of the policies that have been delegated down from the governing board. This is the reason that policy-based governance is used by many large churches that have an average worship attendance of over 400. These churches usually have a senior pastor with three or more additional program staff workers (full-time equivalent).

However, the existence of multiple paid staff members cannot be assumed in a midsize church, and it is highly unlikely in a small church. The parish with an average worship attendance of 150 or fewer usually employs only one ministry worker—the pastor. In the midsize church (150–400 worshipers on average) the pastor is often assisted by a couple of other paid personnel in different full-time and part-time configurations. But the critical mass for a truly staff-managed congregation may not be reached in a midsize church; there remains a need for lay volunteers to manage much of the work of the congregation's ministry and mission.[79] This makes for a very different dynamic than in a truly staff-led church employing multiple paid professional staff workers. Frankly, the volunteer-worker dynamic characteristic of small and midsize congregations is far less adaptive to the use of the Carver model. In fact, organizational consultant James Galvin asserts: "If an organization is volunteer-based and has no paid staff, they simply cannot function as a governing board. . . . For these boards, policy-based governance is out of reach."[80]

Discontented Staff

Some small and midsize congregations that employ few or no paid staff workers have adopted the governing board model. In these cases, the staff is composed of unpaid volunteers who are referred to as "unpaid staff." I have observed, however, persistent unsatisfactory results in such situations. The primary reason this approach does not succeed is because lay volunteers who agree to manage and execute ministry efforts also usually expect to have a voice in the strategic design of that project. They are unwilling to take directives from a higher lay body for their area of responsibility. They see this as a top-down approach. Instead, lay volunteers who offer to serve as congregational leaders or managers also expect to be able to envision its outcomes and to determine its goals from the start. Thus, if a small or midsize congregation employs this model, it must be clearly communicated to the "unpaid staff" that the place of staff workers is only in the operational side of the programmatic efforts of the church, not in the strategic arena, which is the purview of the elected board.

A similar phenomenon can occur even in the case of paid staff. Occasionally, professional staff workers will feel devalued and marginalized under the system of policy-based governance. This is particularly the case when they experience the transition from another organizational structure such as the working or managing models to the Carver model. These program staff workers may complain that they are excluded from making the big strategic decisions for the ministry areas for which they are responsible.

79 See the chapters on pastor, personnel, and participation in David Peter, *Maximizing the Midsize Church*, 87–141.

80 James Galvin, *Maximizing Board Effectiveness*, 48.

Recall that in the governing board model no program staff members sit on the board. The only employee of the congregation to do so is the head pastor (or administrative executive). Thus, the professional ministry staff do not participate directly in the most important decisions that are made for the parish regarding its mission, vision, and goals. They do not have a direct voice in determining the strategic direction of the church and the specific program areas entrusted to them. This can lead to frustration and resentment. A typical complaint goes like this: "I was professionally trained for ministry. I have learned thoroughly the theology, theory, and best practices for leading this aspect of ministry. Yet I have little to no authority in making the major strategic decisions that impact the ministry for which I am responsible. Instead, others who lack the expertise and experience that I have are making those critical decisions."

There is an adage that states, "Authority without accountability is dangerous, and accountability without authority is frustrating." Some professional staff workers functioning under the Carver model experience the frustration of the latter equation. They feel frustrated because they are accountable for ministry where they lack authority to make the most important decisions.

Holding Volunteers Accountable

Speaking of accountability, another issue arises when "unpaid staff" are utilized in this system of governance, as is oftentimes necessary in a midsize church. One of the strengths of the Carver model is its clear lines of accountability. Nevertheless, it is much easier to hold a paid employee accountable for a delegated responsibility than it is to do so with an unpaid volunteer.

When an unpaid staff worker disagrees with any ends or limitations policies that have been handed down for execution, she may simply decide not to comply with those policies. If push comes to shove as a result, the volunteer may resign from the position. The personal cost to do so will probably not be perceived by her as too great; she has simply lost a volunteer position. In the case of a paid staff worker, however, failure to comply with the policies delegated to him will have much more costly ramifications. He could lose his job. This will serve to motivate him to comply with the policies and will make him more accountable. But this motivation of keeping or losing one's source of income is lacking in the case of the unpaid staff worker. Thus, it is more difficult to hold her accountable to the board's directives (i.e., ends and limitations policies).

The Lacuna of Leadership

A significant challenge to the effectiveness of the policy governance model in a congregation of any size is that it requires a highly competent executive pastor. His position is the linchpin of the whole structure, and so if he fails to carry out his responsibilities, then the entire system of governance fails. The truth is that most pastors of midsize churches have not been equipped for this CEO role. Unless they had received a business degree, or picked up executive skills from other life experiences, they will most likely be incapable of handling all the responsibility for administration that is required of them in this model. Ted Kober comments:

> However, most pastors are not trained for CEO management skills, including financial prowess, human resource management (such as recruiting, selecting, and employing staff and working knowledge of human resource laws and processes), business contract law education and experience, property management background, and more. In contrast, pastors are specifically trained *and called* to preach sermons, administer sacraments, teach Bible studies, counsel people biblically, provide spiritual care for people with various life needs, and other ministry relating to Word and Sacrament.[81]

Often pastors who are given the responsibilities that are expected of them in the policy-based governance model will feel like fish out of water. It is not the nature of work for which they prepared themselves. They expected to devote themselves to the study of Scripture, to preaching, to teaching, and to pastoral care. Instead, their job depends upon their ability to execute business.

---

81 Ted Kober, *Policy-Based Board Governance in Lutheran Congregations* (Billings, MT: Ambassadors of Reconciliation, 2008), 4–5.

If the congregation a pastor serves transitions to the Carver model of organization, there is usually a steep learning curve for that pastor, one that is frequently fraught with frustration. Even for those clergy who learn to function under this system, the stress of responsibility can be oppressive. The governing board model requires of the pastor the ability to delegate *all* the programmatic assignments that the ends policies necessitate. And it requires him to hold staff—paid and unpaid—accountable for the results. If the staff workers fail, the senior pastor fails. That is an immense burden for many pastors to bear!

The Secular CEO Syndrome

Another potential peril of this model is that the lead pastor becomes so engaged in his executive and administrative functions that he neglects the spiritual duties assigned to him by God. Holy Scripture emphasizes these responsibilities of pastors: preaching the Gospel, teaching the Word of God, faithfully administering Baptism and the Lord's Supper, nurturing faith, comforting the repentant, disciplining the unrepentant, caring for the hurting, and seeking the lost. These are the priorities of pastoral ministry, as directed by the divine Word. Certainly, administration should be in service to these functions, but it must never usurp them.[82]

According to John Carver's original model, the solution to an incompetent CEO is simply to replace him. If the organization does not produce the results that the board expects of it, then the board has the authority to terminate the CEO and hire a new one with hopes that different results will follow. But there are serious theological and sociological difficulties associated with this approach in the ecclesial context. Most denominational traditions recognize that a pastor cannot be terminated without due cause (such as doctrinal

82 The pastor and ministry staff must not fail to provide spiritual care to the congregation's members. But the congregation also has a responsibility to provide spiritual care to its workers, including the pastor. Ted Kober writes about the use of policy-based governance in churches: "Another effect that we . . . have observed is a lack of spiritual guidance and support for the senior pastor from lay leadership. While not every traditional board of elders fulfills this function properly, most elder boards are given the authority and responsibility to provide spiritual care for their pastors and their families, as well as other called workers. Because the elders' roles are focused on spiritual matters, they can spend more time on studying God's Word together, praying together, and providing spiritual care to the congregation's called workers and their families" (*Policy-Based Board Governance in Lutheran Congregations*, 6).

error or moral failure). Many of these traditions uphold the teaching that a pastor is called to the position by God, and that to remove the pastor from that position involves serious theological implications. In many systems of polity, a lay board is not even authorized to terminate a pastor from his assignment; that must be done either by the voting assembly of the entire church (in a congregational system) or by a bishop (in an episcopal system). Even independent congregations usually hold that the pastoral office is above the "hire and fire" practice of the secular business world.

Board Member Malaise

Not only is the role of the pastor in the Carver model oftentimes difficult to learn but also is the role of the board member. Although it may not always be the most efficient system of organization, the working board model is relatively easy for participants to understand. They intuitively grasp their roles and responsibilities, for they are elected to do the work of the program. In the managing board model, there is a need for more intensive preparation of elected program area directors to assume the role of manager. Yet many can learn the requisite skills, since they involve both hands-on and hands-off activities. But the skills necessary for policy-based governance are rare among most volunteer lay members of a church. Yet these are the people who are elected to fill the governing board.

The primary work of the governing board is to write policies (ends and limitations) that direct the strategic goals of the congregation and the legal, ethical, prudential, and financial boundaries in which those goals will be pursued. Doing this kind of board work is not intuitive, nor is it easy. It takes training to be a capable board member, but oftentimes such training is omitted or woefully inadequate. When appropriate training is provided to new board members, some may become jaded to their role. James Galvin observes a fairly common response: "Some board members, upon learning about how to write policies, exclaim, 'I didn't come on to this board to do this crud!' Of course not, they came on to exert control over the organization by making operational decisions."[83]

83 Galvin, "The Great Board Debate," 9.

Not only must the board learn what it *should* do but it also must learn what it should *not* do. This means that board members must stay out of managing the ministry of the congregation. They must abstain from involvement in operational matters. They must not get involved in staff work. In theory, that may sound appealing. But in reality, most people can conceptualize ministry only—or mostly—at a concrete and operational level. This is why board members will habitually veer into discussions of operations. I have observed this tendency even among highly qualified members of governing boards. I have observed this tendency in myself! Some of the governance boards in which I have participated have in fact appointed a "board marshal" to blow the whistle when board members move from the work of governance to the work of management. For most of us, carrying out responsibilities as a board member in the Carver model goes against our natural inclinations. Many church boards, while attracted to the theory of policy-based governance with its clear lines of accountability and potential efficiencies, simply cannot make it happen in practice.

This means that if a church decides to adopt the Carver model for its organizational structure, its leaders and members will most likely need to be tutored through the transition. If there is a transition from the working board model or from the managing board model, there will need to be as much unlearning of the old model as there is learning of the new. Some books will aid in this process. Of course, the resources from John Carver can be helpful. But even better are books that apply the model directly to use in a faith-based congregation. Of these, I recommend *Winning on Purpose: How to Organize Congregations to Succeed in Their Mission* by John Kaiser; *Governance and Ministry: Rethinking Board Leadership* by Dan Hotchkiss; and *Structure Your Church for Mission* by Kurt Bickel and Les Stroh. In moving to the board governance model, it is best that someone leads the transition who has significant experience and expertise in policy-based governance.

WEIGHING THE VALUE OF THE GOVERNING BOARD MODEL

There are potential benefits to functioning with a governing board. There are also significant challenges. And these are not unrelated to congregational size. A large church will probably consider adopting some revision of the Carver model. In a small church, it most likely won't work. The midsize parish is in that middle ground where the model may or may not succeed. If any church decides to adopt the policy-based governance model, it should receive guidance to do so and make necessary adaptations that accord with its distinctive context. It should endeavor to maximize the strengths of this model and seek to avoid its problematic aspects.

PART III:

IMPROVING ORGANIZATION IN THE CHURCH

Most organizational structures used by North American churches employ some incarnation of one of the three board models—working, managing, governing—featured in the previous chapters. Although these models have common features and seek a common goal of advancing the kingdom of God, there are significant differences, as has been described. Yet there are some principles and practices that churches can apply for the benefit of mission and ministry no matter what their structural model is. These best practices can be used with the traditional council model (working board), the streamlined administrative model (managing board), and the corporate policy-based model (governing board). The final chapters of this book will describe how to apply them to each model.

Chapter 7 presents the strategy of using action teams to accomplish the goals and responsibilities of a church. These entities are as their title indicates—teams of volunteers who assemble to *act* upon a specific effort to accomplish the task assigned to them. They are focused, short term, task oriented, and accountable. All three models of boards—working, managing, governing—can utilize action teams to execute their objectives and to move forward in ministry. Chapter 7 further describes

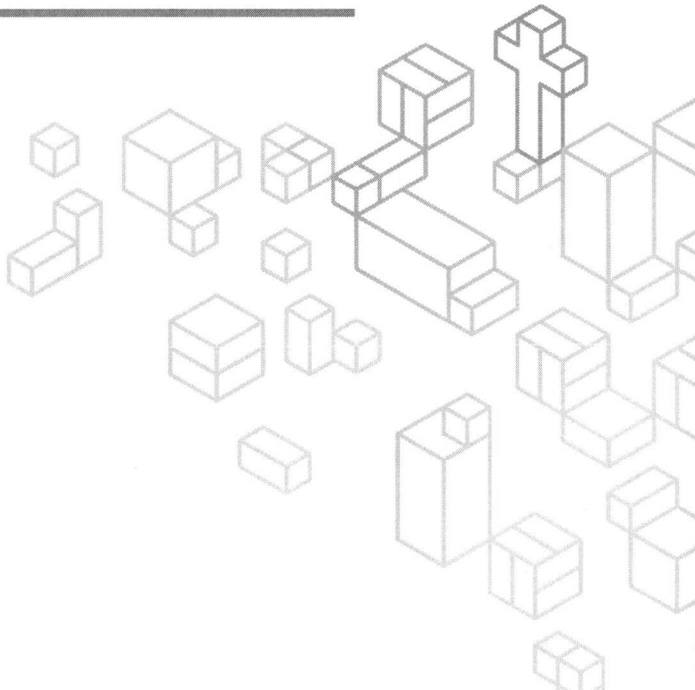

how to form action teams and employ them in varying contexts at the operational level of a congregation's work.

Chapters 8 and 9 are concerned more specifically with identifying and developing leaders who will fill some board positions. As such, these chapters address not so much the doers of the congregation's work (operations) but the leaders of the doers (management and governance). Chapter 8 focuses on forming competent board leaders through an equipping process of instruction, immersion, and imitation. Chapter 9 presents a method for empowering board leaders to innovate in changing times and conditions. In both chapters, the methodology is applied to the varying models so that the reader may appropriate what is useful to his or her church's organizational structure.

The final chapter (10) identifies ways to integrate spiritual practices into board business. By engaging in these Spirit-led activities, lay leaders will experience spiritual nurture and growth during their term of service. These practices entail learning from God's Word, telling stories of God's work, and praying for God's blessing. As they integrate spiritual dynamics into the business of organizing the congregation, board members find fulfillment and a deepening of their faith.

CHAPTER 7

DEVELOPING **ACTION TEAMS**

Churches in the United States and Canada typically organize around one of three board models—working, managing, and governing. The members of these boards are elected to their positions by the congregation at large, usually through its congregational assembly. As such, they are regarded as lay officers of the church. The parish entrusts to them the responsibility to carry out its purposes effectively and faithfully.

These officers gather in what are called standing boards because the boards are permanent fixtures in the organizational life of the congregation. Their status as *standing* indicates that they are to remain in place into perpetuity. Their permanence reflects the church's commitment to continue the causes to which they attend. For example, a congregation's bylaws may prescribe that it has boards for Christian education, worship, and outreach because it regards education, worship, and outreach to be ongoing priorities. In the case of policy-based governance, a church's constitution may stipulate that it must always have a board of directors because it regards lay governance to be necessary. Each of these is a standing board. The board models that have been described in the previous three chapters all assume this standing status.

But there is another aspect of organization that is increasingly useful in churches. It does not require any standing status. This organizational unit does not require any permanent prescription within the constitution or bylaws. It does not insist that group members be formally elected by the plenary congregation. Participants are not expected to serve during set terms of two or three years. This group arises informally and sometimes spontaneously. It is flexible and nimble. And it can be very effective in accomplishing significant work in the name of the congregation. This entity is an *action team.* Action teams complement and supplement standing boards. Actually, standing boards will do well to utilize action teams in the execution of their responsibilities.

ANATOMY OF AN ACTION TEAM

Most people are familiar with teams by either participating in or watching team sports such as baseball, basketball, or soccer. But teams can also be useful in the organizational life of businesses, nonprofit organizations, and even churches. A team is a group of people who collaborate to advance a common purpose and achieve shared goals. Each team member brings distinctive abilities to the collective whole and is accountable to the other members in fulfilling assigned responsibilities.[84]

In the church context, teams are best kept small, ideally no more than six members.[85] Participants are selected and recruited because they demonstrate complementary aptitudes for accomplishing a shared goal. The word *complementary* does not mean the same aptitudes are shared by all members of the team, but that diverse skills and giftedness are valued as long as they interact harmoniously.[86] A team commits to a shared purpose and goals, which become the focus of its efforts and energy (similar to a football team committed to scoring touchdowns and winning the game). Finally, teammates hold one another accountable to the expectations they have for each participant.

---

84 For a more complete analysis of teams, see Jon Katzenbach and Douglas Smith, *The Wisdom of Teams: Creating the High-Performance Organization* (Boston: Harvard Business School Press, 1993), 45.

85 Brian Hughes maintains that although single-cell groups can function with as many as eight people, the optimal size is six people. See Brian Hughes, *Our Structure: Carrying Out the Vision* (Minneapolis: Augsburg-Fortress, 2002), 71–72. George Barna asserts that effective teams have three to five members and should never exceed six participants. See George Barna, *The Power of Team Leadership* (Colorado Springs: Waterbrook Press, 2001), 24.

86 George Barna recommends four aptitudes be present among the members of a team: directing, strategic, team-building, and operational skills. Barna, *The Power of Team Leadership,* 99–113.

In many ways, the boards that were described in the previous chapters may fit this definition of a team. Ideally that will be the case, as the board members collaborate to accomplish the objectives that have been assigned to them in the congregation's constitution and bylaws or by the directive of the congregational assembly. What distinguishes the action teams from these standing boards is that they are constituted to accomplish a given specific task, and once that task is completed, the team disbands. The fact that these are called *action* teams also points to their ad hoc purpose. The members of the action team are gathered and authorized to *act* to accomplish a specific task or directive.

When do action teams come into play in the organizational work of a congregation? Essentially, action teams arise when action is needed. They are formed to do work that the church deems necessary and important. An action team might assemble to execute Vacation Bible School one summer. A team might gather to coordinate a monthly meal at a community homeless center. The action team may be tasked with refurbishing classrooms in the educational wing of the church. A team could coordinate the fund-raising effort so that teens in the congregation can attend a youth gathering. Each of these is an example of the ad hoc nature of action teams. The actual responsibilities of any given action team depend on the needs and directives of the congregation that it serves.

ADDED VALUE

Action teams can supplement the impact of a standing board and complement that board's efforts. Accordingly, these teams add value to the organizational productivity of a congregation. Action teams will almost always function in the operational dimension of parish activity, whereas standing boards may only function in the managerial or supervisory dimension (governance). But this operational dynamic is essential because it is where the work actually gets done. It is where execution of ministry initiatives occurs at the concrete level.

Here are some of the benefits of action teams that make them so valuable to congregational lay service:

- Action teams get work done. They convene to accomplish a task, and their singular focus is the achievement of the task. Their purpose is to affect a desired outcome and produce a desired result, and teammates find fulfillment when these goals are achieved.
- Action teams usually involve a short-term commitment. When the assigned task is completed, the team celebrates the accomplishment and disbands. The team therefore has a temporary lifespan— usually of no more than a few months. Rarely does an action team function for more than a year. A benefit of this is that most busy lay members are more willing to invest themselves into short-term projects rather than long-term positions.
- Action teams enable people to focus on their interests. Typically, the outcome produced by an action team is singular and narrow, whereas the objectives of a standing board are multiple and broad. Accordingly, people devote themselves to more specific interests in action teams that align closely with what they are most interested in and committed to. They focus on specific causes for which they have a passion.
- Action teams distribute the work that the congregation deems important. No one board or governance body is expected to do all the work of a congregation, and action teams provide a mechanism by which that work can be shared by many in the congregation. The adage that "many hands make light work" applies in that many action teams disperse and distribute the burden of responsibility to more and more people.
- Action teams provide opportunity for engagement in ministry involving a wider pool of participants. Not everyone has the gifts and temperament to serve in a standing working board. Even fewer are equipped to function as managers in the managing board model or as directors in a governing board model. But most church volunteers can find a place to serve in an action team.

HOW THE THREE MODELS USE ACTION TEAMS

Each of the three models of board governance described in Part 2 may benefit by using action teams. Here is how the working, managing, and governing models integrate the use of these teams.

Working Board Application

A working board may execute action teams to advance the work that has been assigned to it. Recall that the members of a working board have been elected to directly do the work of ministry. But this doesn't mean the working board is the only team to carry out the work. The board may organize action teams to collaborate with it.

This can be illustrated with a typical working board, the board of Christian education. This board is composed of six members, each of whom have a special area of oversight. One member is responsible for the children's Sunday School ministry. Another sees to the adult education program. A third member coordinates the annual Vacation Bible School, and a fourth coordinates the parish's home Bible study groups. The fifth board worker serves as the church librarian. The last board member is the director of the board.

It would be inefficient and less productive if the six members of this board were the only ones in the parish who do the work of teaching and leading Sunday School, adult education, Vacation Bible School, and home Bible study, and doing library maintenance. They would likely become exhausted from the work, fail to get it all done, or both. In addition, by restricting the work to themselves, they would deprive others from using their gifts to promote Christian education in the congregation.

Instead, others are involved in action teams. The board member who is responsible for Sunday School could assemble an action team that serves as the teaching faculty. The adult education coordinator might gather an action team to assist in planning courses, selecting curriculum, recruiting instructors, and offering classes for adults. The VBS director forms a team to execute the week-long summer program. The home Bible study coordinator manages the hosts of these home studies, who function as a de facto team. Even the church librarian might assemble a small team to assist in keeping track of the church's books and resources, although this may be manageable for one person.

This use of action teams by a working board will result in many benefits to the local congregation. First, the work assigned to the board gets done, which is the primary purpose of the working board. Second, productivity is multiplied by the participation of many. Third, more congregational members are involved, which gives them opportunity to exercise their giftedness and service to others; this in turn integrates them into more active membership in the church. Action teams can be a potent supplement to the working board model.

Managing Board Application

If a congregation adopts the managing board model of organization, it is practically essential that it utilize action teams. Indeed, such teams are a *sine qua non* of this approach to church management.

In the managing board model, the primary role of the elected lay members is to manage. This assumes that these elected officers must manage something or someone. The "something" that these members manage are ministry areas, and the "someone" who are managed are volunteer workers. An effective way of organizing these volunteers is into action teams. As such, the elective officer in this structure essentially manages multiple action teams in her program area.

This can be illustrated with a typical managing board, which includes a director (and an assistant) for each of the following age-oriented program areas: children's ministry, youth/young adult ministry, and adult ministry. The manager of the children's ministry has, in collaboration with his assistant, identified five strategic efforts for this program area. The manager then recruits leaders for each of these efforts, assists them in forming action teams, provides resources and support for these teams, and supervises their efforts to assure that they are effective and ethical. The first action team focuses on developing the weekly Sunday morning children's education hour. The second team collaborates to offer occasional children's messages in the worship services. The third team executes the annual week-long Vacation Bible School. The fourth team organizes the church-sponsored Trunk-or-Treat outreach to the neighborhood around Halloween. A fifth team organizes two annual retreats, one for fathers and sons and the other for mothers and daughters, to prepare middle-school kids for adolescence. The actual execution of each of these strategic efforts is accomplished by the action teams. But the children's ministry manager and her assistant, function as catalyzers and overseers of all the teams. They carry out their roles as managers of others who are constituted into action teams.

Governing Board Application

Action teams have a place in the organization of a parish that is administered by policy-based governance. But in this system, the governing board, such as a board of directors, should never engage directly with action teams. One of the fundamental principles of policy-based governance as espoused by John Carver is the clean separation of governance from operations. Governing boards should attend to governance only. They should not get into the weeds of operations. But action teams by their very nature fall into the realm of operations. *Action*, from the Latin word *actio*, meaning "to do," equates closely with *operation*, from the Latin *operari*, meaning "to work." These teams are to enact the work of the parish at an operational level.

Accordingly, there is an intermediary level between governance—which is the realm of the governing board—and operations, which is the realm of the action teams. The intervening entity is the professional church staff. In the governing model, the board delegates to the staff directives in the form of ends and limitations policies. These policies are then implemented by the staff members, who report back to the board regarding their compliance to the policies. Accordingly, execution of the work of the parish is the responsibility of the professional staff (pastors, teaching professionals, cantors, youth directors, outreach coordinators, etc.), who in effect function as managers accountable to the governing board.

In the governing model of church organization, the use of action teams therefore falls under the purview of the professional staff, not the governing board. The staff workers form action teams to accomplish the tasks assigned to them by the board of directors. Recall the following graphic used to depict the structure of policy-based governance:

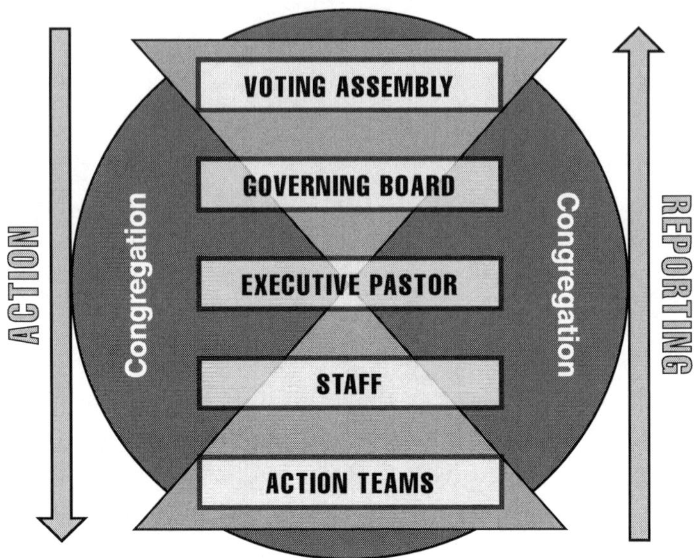

Note that in this diagram, the staff are positioned in the level immediately above the action teams. So the staff directly gather, form, manage, and resource these teams. Staff delegate action items to the teams, and the action teams report to their respective staff members but not to the governing board.

A demonstration of how action teams can be utilized in a policy-based governance structure builds on the example narrated in the previous chapter. Recall that the governing board of the church, the board of directors, established the ends policy that at least three international mission trips be sponsored by the congregation. The limitations policies delineated the funding of these mission trips and the safety of the participants. The senior pastor delegated the ends and limitations policies to the staff person overseeing missions. This staff worker in turn recruited lay participants for the three mission teams. These mission teams functioned as action teams. One team organized to build a residence in Mexico, another led an eyeglass clinic in Belize, and a third undertook to dig a well in Uganda. The director of missions, the congregation's professional staff person, served as the manager of these action teams by recruiting leaders, equipping them for their service, training them in cultural awareness and personal safety, communicating with the host sites, and assisting with resources for each trip.

All of this is done within the bounds of the ends and limitations policies that were composed by the governing board. The governing board hears the report of each mission trip from the senior pastor (who has received that report from the staff worker). But the board in no way manages these teams or directs them. This illustrates how action teams may be beneficially utilized within the governing board model.

FORMING ACTION TEAMS

Action teams have the potential to accomplish significant work within the organizational structure of a Christian congregation. But how are these developed? What efforts need to be undertaken to form action teams? Basically, four steps contribute to the formation of these teams.

Assignment. The first step is to *assign* a leader. In other words, start with an individual, not a group. Church consultant Kennon Callahan maintains that it is better to start with a leader who is passionate about a cause and allow him to assemble a team than to start with a team and hope it appoints a capable leader.[87] So the first thing to do is to find someone to lead the project. Search for and discover someone who has a passion for the cause and who is competent to lead the effort. Identify who might best promote the cause and ask her to lead it. It is the responsibility of the director in the managing model or the staff person in the governing model to identify and recruit a leader, not an entire team, to head up the effort. Early on, it is critical to communicate to this leader what the desired outcomes are (ends) as well as what restrictions and resources are in place for the endeavor (limitations).

Assembly. The second step is to *assemble* a team. The person who has been recruited to lead the team does the assembling, not the standing board. This person identifies and recruits others to join her in the cause. She is authorized to build her own team. If she has passion about this project, she will likely know others who share those longings. An official from the standing board (board member, manager, staff worker) may give counsel and guidance, but it is the newly minted leader's role to

87 Kennon Callahan, *Effective Church Leadership: Building on the Twelve Keys* (San Francisco: Jossey-Bass, 1997), 211.

gather a team to work with her. Typically, the optimal number for an action team is four to six members, so this leader should be encouraged to assemble three to five others to assist her. These additional team members are selected both for their passion for the cause and their competence in executing it. Furthermore, teams composed of members with varying gifts and aptitudes typically produce better results.

Assistance. The third step in forming an action team is to *assist* its efforts. This means to provide the necessary direction and resources for accomplishing its assigned task. Assistance may be given in setting team goals, identifying operating guidelines, and developing the work plan. For example, in the case of a policy-based governance system, the staff person gives direction by providing the team with the appropriate ends and limitations policies. This staff person identifies what monetary resources are available from the church's budget. He may also assist the team by offering other resources such as the congregation's facilities, media, and communication network. The staff person avails himself as a consultant on an as-needed basis.

Assessment. The fourth and final step in the process is to *assess* the action team's efforts. This assessment is done at the midway point and at the end of the team's tenure of activity. The earlier assessment allows for any course correction that may be needed. The final assessment provides a summary evaluation of the team's efforts. The basis for the assessment is the accomplishment of the outcomes (ends) that were initially assigned to the team. Assessment also reviews how well the team conformed to any applied restrictions or policies (limitations) as well as how the team stewarded the resources it received. The overseeing board or staff worker performs the assessment. This review allows the team participants to celebrate successes and learn from shortfalls. It enables the supervising official to affirm the team's accomplishments and appreciate its efforts. Finally, all who are involved may give thanks and glory to God for His mighty work accomplished in and through this action team.

SUMMARY

Action teams can be valuable assets to the organizational structure of the local congregation. When done well, they are focused and productive. They typically require short-term commitments from participants, which is more conducive to the schedules of busy church members. They enable a high proportion of laypeople in a church to be active in ministry by using their gifts in causes about which they are passionate.

Each of the three basic models of church organization may utilize action teams to advance its purposes. In the working board model, the board itself may function as an action team or recruit other teams to support its work. Action teams are for the most part essential to the operation of the managing board model, since the elected managers are to organize others into teams to get the work done. Although the board of directors in the governing board model does not engage directly with action teams, the policies composed by the board trickle down to teams for execution. All three organizational models benefit from using action teams.

Action teams are formed by following a process that involves assignment, assembly, assistance, and assessment. This process allows for appropriate autonomy of the team while also holding it accountable for its appointed tasks.

CHAPTER 8

FORMING **COMPETENT** BOARD **LEADERS**

In previous chapters, we considered options for congregational organization. Three dominant models of organizational structure were examined—working, managing, and governing boards. We also investigated how lay action teams can be utilized in each of these models. But a critical dynamic is necessary for any of these approaches to work. There needs to be good *lay leadership* for the boards and action teams to function effectively and productively.

EQUIPPING LAY LEADERS

The development of lay leadership does not occur automatically and usually not intuitively. It requires very intentional thinking and acting. The adage rings true—leaders are made, not born. Leaders must be equipped and formed. Pastors seek, in Paul's words, to "equip the saints for the work of ministry, for building up the body of Christ" (Ephesians 4:12).

In the New Testament, the early leaders of the Church were prepared for their leadership roles through intentional processes of formation. The twelve disciples received three years of instruction by Jesus and immersion in His ministry before being sent forth for mission on the day of Pentecost (Luke 24:44–49). After his dramatic conversion, Paul spent several years preparing himself and interacting with Christian leaders before embarking on his first missionary journey under the leadership of his mentor, Barnabas (Galatians 1:15–21). Later, Paul mentored Timothy during two missionary journeys before settling the young protégé as a pastor in Ephesus (Acts 16:1–5; 17:14–15; 20:4–5; Romans 16:21; 2 Corinthians 1:19; 1 Timothy 1:3; 2 Timothy 1:3–7, 13–14; 2:1–3; 3:10–17). This process of forming leaders for Christ's ministry and mission has rich precedent in the practice of Jesus and of the Early Church.

An emerging lay leader needs to be equipped for the leadership role that he assumes. He learns how to lead in the specific context of his board or action team. The Church is to equip its nascent leaders for the responsibilities assigned to them. They are to gain information about, experience with, and expertise in the functions of leadership. This process of leadership formation involves learning and practice.

Three dynamics interact in this equipping process: instruction, immersion, and imitation.[88] These dynamics follow a logical progression, but they are not completely sequential. The leadership formation process is a recursive one. Each of these dynamics will heretofore be identified and explained. They are illustrated by the leadership formation process for young Timothy, the protégé of the apostle Paul. Then they are also applied to the working, managing, and governing board models used in churches today.

INSTRUCTION

Instruction is vital to most formation processes. This is why most societies value education. Instruction is a critical ingredient to the formation of Christian leaders. Paul states that becoming "a good servant of Christ Jesus" results from "being trained in the words of the faith and of the good doctrine" (1 Timothy 4:6).

Such instruction is delivered in formal educational institutions such as seminaries, Christian colleges, and Bible schools. But it is also important in the context of the local congregation. Catechesis in Scripture and doctrine grounds believers in the faith. Biblical and doctrinal instruction forms spiritually mature leaders; it helps them

88 The equivalent of two of these dynamics—information (instruction) and imitation—is developed in Mike Breen, *Multiplying Missional Leaders: From Half-Hearted Volunteers to a Mobilized Kingdom Force* (Pawleys Island, SC: 3dm, 2012), 83–84.

to understand the *what* and *why* of ministry. Instruction in leadership theory and methods prepares lay volunteers for the ministry of leading. This provides them with insight into methods and programmatic design, the *how* of ministry.

One of the most important aspects of instruction for leadership is to provide information about the responsibilities that the layperson will assume. He is duly familiarized with the desired expectations and outcomes of his participation in congregational leadership. He becomes acquainted with the church's policies and procedures that guide its operations.

Various modes of delivering this instruction exist. Information can be delivered face-to-face, in a group setting, online using prerecorded video sessions, and via other venues. Often, reading resources support it. Some information may be theological in nature. Other material may be more practical in the sense of providing a how-to guide. The result is that the new leader understands his assigned responsibilities and knows how to accomplish them.

It is clear that the apostle Paul provided ample instruction to Timothy in their mentoring relationship. Paul instructed Timothy in the content of Scripture and in sound doctrine, preparing him for the theological nature of his calling (1 Timothy 1:3; 2 Timothy 1:13–14; 3:14–17). Moreover, Paul's two epistles to Timothy show that the apostle continued to instruct his protégé not only in Christian doctrine but especially in the practice of ministry. This includes how to deal with false teachers and troublemakers (1 Timothy 1:3–11; 4:1–16; 6:3–16; 20–21; 2 Timothy 2:14–3:9), how to lead prayer and worship (1 Timothy 2:1–15), how to choose other leaders (1 Timothy 3:1–13; 5:17–22; 2 Timothy 2:1–2), how to practice care for needy people like widows (1 Timothy 5:1–16), and how to preach and teach (1 Timothy 4:6–16; 2 Timothy 3:14–17; 4:1–5).

INSTRUCTION APPLIED TO ORGANIZATIONAL MODELS

The dynamic of learning is critical to leadership formation in each of the models of organizational structure described previously. In the working board model, the ministry-program board directors (such as the chairman of the worship board) will be the primary leaders. In the managing board model, the leaders are the program-area managers and their assistants. In the governing board model, the leaders are members of the board of directors who formulate policies for the congregation.

Fundamental to the instruction of church leaders is formation in the Word of God. Ideally, recruits to leadership positions will already demonstrate a devotion to learning from the Scriptures. Indeed, this is an appropriate prerequisite to church leadership. Church leaders should participate in at least one Bible study or ongoing Christian education activity. Being a student of the Word of God is a given for those who lead His people.

New leaders should also be instructed in the mission of God (*missio dei*) and the Lord's purposes and priorities as presented in the Bible. This is to assure that their leadership aligns with God's mission. Furthermore, they should learn what the congregation's distinctive missional direction is by becoming orientated to its stated mission, vision, values, and strategic priorities.

One of the first pieces of information to be provided to the new leader under any model regards his accountability and authority.[89] This information is essential for the leader to function effectively.

Information about *accountability* will identify to whom the new leader is accountable (i.e., the lines of accountability), but it will do much more than this. It will especially address the intended *outcomes* ("ends") for the area of his oversight—that is, the strategic goals and hoped-for fruit of his efforts. These broad objectives may be articulated in some written form that has been officially approved by the congregation. They may be in the church's bylaws, the parish's strategic plan,

89 Paul reminds Timothy of his authority in 1 Timothy 4:11–16 and of his accountability in 2 Timothy 2:1, 4:1.

or some other document. They may simply have been written by the pastor or program-staff person to whom the lay leader is accountable. This will help the emerging leader to understand the expectations that the parish has for the leadership position. It will also enable him to envision the destination to which his leadership role should lead and to embrace its significance and potential impact.

The working board model employs a system of standing boards. As such, these boards usually have objectives that are stated in an official written document of the congregation, such as the bylaws or a procedures manual. In such a case, the board director should become familiar with these objectives. The managing board model is similar in that the ministry area to which the manager is assigned frequently has some official description and list of desired outcomes that he may study and act on. In the case of the governing board model, the elected members of the board should be instructed about their responsibilities and should become thoroughly familiar with the existing written ends policies as well as the policies for board governance and executive linkage.[90] All of this requires instruction.

The emerging leader will also acquaint himself with the *authority* that is entrusted to his position of leadership. He will learn how the congregation authorizes him to lead. This can be articulated in various limitations policies for the position. Most significant in this regard is to communicate what resources—finances, facilities, communication modes, program-staff expertise, and so forth—are at the leader's disposal. For example, in the case of the chairperson of the youth board, one resource is the support and guidance of the called staff person, such as the director of education and youth. The financial resources would be specified in the budget for the youth board, facility resources are located primarily in the youth room, and the human resources would include board members, volunteer youth counselors, and parents.

90 James Galvin advocates a thorough orientation of new members of a governing board. He writes: "As new trustees are voted onto the governing board, they need an on-boarding process to help them understand policy-based governance, the existing board policy manual, and how the board functions. This packet can include a copy of the board policy manual, a book to read about policy-based governance, and articles from the internet. Before their first board meeting, schedule a meeting with a couple of experienced board members to answer any questions they may have. This way the new board members will be able to contribute productively from their first meeting instead of a waiting and watching for a couple of months to 'see how things are done around here.'" James Galvin, *Five Types of Governance*, p. 14.

Other limitations policies for the position might include ethical and legal issues. An ethical policy for the youth board to oversee is that an adult counselor is never to be alone with a teenager. A legal policy is that background checks are made on all volunteers who work with the youth.

In the working board model, each board director should be instructed regarding the board's budget, program staff, legal and ethical boundaries, and modes for communication. The same is true in the case of the director and assistant manager in the managing board system. In policy-based governance, each member of the board of directors is informed about the existing limitations policies and the reasons behind these. These are all ways in which the emerging lay leaders become familiar with the authority vested in their positions.

The leader and his team have great freedom and latitude to carry out their assigned responsibilities and vision within these boundaries. That is where the authority lies—within the parameters of the limitations established by the congregation for the position.

Finally, instruction in the subject of leadership itself may be worthwhile. There are many resources available in this regard. I have also found helpful introductions to the basic nature of leadership, as applied in a Christian context, in the books *Christian Reflections on the Leadership Challenge, Church Leadership,* and *I've Got Your Back.*[91] Tim Elmore's series titled *Habitudes* provides useful insights into leadership for lay workers.[92] In the case of new members of the board of directors serving in the governing model, they can read about policy-based governance in books such as *Winning on Purpose, Governance and Ministry,* and *Structure Your Church for Mission.*[93] Resources such as these help to orient emerging leaders to the nature of their leadership role.

91 James M. Kouzes and Barry Z. Posner, *Christian Reflections on the Leadership Challenge* (San Francisco: Jossey-Bass, 2004); Lovett H. Weems, *Church Leadership*, rev. ed. (Nashville: Abingdon Press, 2010); James Galvin, *I've Got Your Back: Biblical Principles for Leading and Following Well* (Elgin, IL: Tenth Power, 2012).

92 Tim Elmore, *Habitudes: Images That Form Leadership Habits and Attitudes* (Atlanta: Growing Leaders Inc., 2006–2009).

93 Kaiser, *Winning on Purpose* (Nashville: Abingdon Press 2006); Hotchkiss, *Governance and Ministry* (Lanham: Rowman & Littlefield Publishers, 2009); Bickel and Stroh, *Structure Your Church for Mission* (Strobican Publishing LLC, 2010)..

The need to be instructed for the leadership task is most critical early in the learning process. But it continues throughout the formation process. Good leaders, and those who follow them, are constantly learning as they receive new information. The leader will seek out and welcome useful instruction at all times.

IMMERSION

The process of equipping lay leaders involves another dynamic beyond the acquisition of information through instruction. It is the observation of leadership in practice. It is the engagement with field experience. One of the best ways to learn leadership skills is in the context of practice-reflection.

This is the dynamic of *immersion* in which potential leaders are immersed in the assigned effort. They best learn the culture and values of the congregation's ministry by being immersed in the workings of its programs and processes. They gain insight into significant traditions and practices. As emerging leaders are immersed in the work of ministry, their engagement with leadership is transformed from theory to practice. That makes a significant difference! The nature of leadership may be taught through instruction, but it is caught in the immersive experience.

This immersive dynamic can be compared to the process of learning to swim. A person acquires this ability by being placed in water, of course with close supervision. Learning to swim necessitates being immersed in water. Similarly, nascent leaders will best learn how to function in leadership by being immersed in the activity—simply by doing it. There will need to be some supervision and on-site direction by veteran leaders. Leaders are developed not only in the classroom where information is obtained but also—even especially—in the field where experience is gained. This on-the-job training is essential to forming competent lay leaders.

Young Timothy was immersed in the experience of mission work from the very start of his participation with Paul's ministry. One of the very first things said in Scripture of this emerging leader is that "Paul wanted Timothy to accompany him" (Acts 16:3). It was by being in the company of Paul and his missionary companions that Timothy learned about the realities of mission work. Timothy observed that there were many hardships as well as much joy in ministry and experienced such trials and delights in the immersive journey. Timothy accompanied Paul in the apostle's second and third missionary trips and beyond (Acts 16:3–4; 17:14–15; 18:5–6; 20:4–5; Philippians 1:1; Colossians 1:1). These immersion experiences had a profound formative influence on the young leader and prepared him well for his ministry apart from Paul.

IMMERSION APPLIED TO ORGANIZATIONAL MODELS

The dynamic of immersion is critical to learning to lead. Each of the three models of organization can apply it to their leadership formation processes.

Working Board Application

In the working board model, the immersive experience involves climbing the ladder of experience. Nelson Searcy calls this the ministry ladder.[94] The strategy is that volunteers climb the ladder of ministry experience to higher levels of leadership. For example, before assuming the role of director of the board of Christian education, Sally will have progressed from Sunday School aide to teacher to superintendent, which is a position on the education board. Then, having been immersed in the workings of this board for at least a term, she is ready to assume responsibility as leader of the board (board director) if she demonstrates the requisite competence. This immersive journey equips her to navigate successfully the culture, expectations, roles, and responsibilities associated with the leadership positions toward the top of the ladder.

Managing Board Application

The immersion dynamic is intentionally hardwired into the managing board model if it employs the use of assistant managers. The assistant works alongside the lead director and is given assignments for management as necessary. The result is that the assistant receives on-the-job

94 Nelson Searcy, *Connect: How to Double Your Number of Volunteers* (Grand Rapids: Baker Books, 2012), 105.

training to eventually become the director. The assistant is immersed in the management functions as she collaborates with the lead manager.

The assistant is immersed not only in the functions of managing the distinct ministry program area to which she is assigned, such as youth ministry. She is also familiarized with her program area's linkage to the larger congregational system as she attends some of the regular administrative council meetings. Here she sees how her distinctive ministry area interfaces with other ministry areas such as children's ministry, worship, education, and outreach.

In this manner, the assistant observes and integrates leadership and management skills in the immersive apprenticeship process. This equips her for higher levels of leadership in the future.

Governing Board Application

The governing model is the most challenging context in which to maximize the immersion dynamic. This is because there is no process in this model that is comparable to the ministry ladder (used in the working model) or the apprenticeship approach (used in the managing model). Nevertheless, the immersion dynamic can be applied. The first way to do this is to recruit members of the board who already have experience with policy-based governance in their vocations. Many professionals in business, government, education, and the military are familiar with this approach as they have served on boards that employ the Carver method. But admittedly, this pool of candidates will be small in most congregations.

The second method is to distinguish between senior and junior members of the board. The junior members are those who have been on the board for less than a set time period, such as six months. During this introductory period, the junior members attend board meetings simply to observe and to learn the ropes of policy-based governance. Gradually, they move into more active participation in the policy-making processes of the board as they become familiar with its operations through immersion.

Future lay leaders will benefit from immersion in ministry before taking the reins of primary leadership. Immersion in the context of the actual practice of leadership is an effective proving ground for leadership formation.

IMITATION

The practice of imitation is an important component of the leadership formation process. Throughout history, people in many cultures have learned skills through apprenticeships. This is the tradition for training in trades such as carpentry, plumbing, and electrical. But it is also an effective approach for developing leaders in the professions, in government, and in education. This occurs in the context of internships involving student teachers, medical residents, law clerks, congressional aides, and seminary interns. Examples of this dynamic in popular fiction include the Padawan, who prepare to become Jedi knights in the Star Wars series, and Harry Potter, who at his matriculation at Hogwarts is assigned by the Sorting Hat to "Apprenticeship." Oftentimes, the word *mentorship* is used to describe this process. In the New Testament, the concept of *discipleship* captures this dynamic.

In many ways, this was the *modus operandi* of Jesus in His strategy to raise up leaders. The apostles were the primary leaders He appointed to continue His mission after His ascension. Yet He formed them to be leaders by inviting them to join Him in His earthly ministry, calling them to follow Him (Matthew 4:19; Mark 1:17; 2:14; Luke 5:27; John 1:43). For at least three years, they accompanied Him and lived with Him, observing His public ministry and engaging in private discourse with Him. It is clear that Jesus employed the practice-reflection approach in training the Twelve (e.g., Luke 10:1–24). But He especially modelled for them God-pleasing attitudes and behaviors for carrying out ministry and mission. The call to imitate Christ is evident in several of the discourses that He shared with His disciples toward the end of the three-year formation period (Matthew 16:24; 20:25–28; Luke 22:25–27; John 13:12–20; 33–35; 20:21).

Similarly, the apostle Paul exhorted his protégé, Timothy, to follow his example of missional leadership. Paul challenged his spiritual son: "Follow the pattern of the sound words that you have heard from me, in the faith and love that are in Christ Jesus" (2 Timothy 1:13). He also commends Timothy, saying, "You . . . have followed my teaching, my conduct, my aim in life, my faith, my patience, my love, my steadfastness" (2 Timothy 3:10). Paul affirmed the practice of imitation in the leadership formation of his apprentice missionary and pastor.

Organizations engage the dynamic of imitation when an experienced leader models leadership skills and practices. The emerging leader, the apprentice, observes the attitudes and behavior of the mentor and integrates these into her own efforts toward leadership. She observes how her mentor operates and imitates that behavior. She practices limited leadership in partnership with and under the guidance of another more experienced leader. The result is that the apprentice is prepared for greater responsibility when released to lead, thus replicating leadership.

Imitation is a powerful means for people to learn skills. It is the "watch, learn, and try" approach, involving observation and integration. The YouTube phenomenon illustrates this well. When someone undertakes a DIY home or auto repair project, the person oftentimes views a YouTube video that demonstrates how the repair is performed. Having observed the demonstration, the aspiring handyman imitates the effort at home. Similarly, a person experiments with a new recipe by watching the steps of preparation online. Skills in the arts and athletics can be acquired this way too.

Although this virtual approach to imitation is helpful for many endeavors, in many situations, I find it best to access a skilled practitioner who is present to guide and direct me. He shows me how to get started and then guides me as I do some of the work. When he observes that I have gained the needed skill, my friend departs. Yet I continue the project. I progress because I am imitating my friend's technique. In the end, I find satisfaction not only in successfully getting the job done but also in having gained the skills that I continue to employ in the future.

Not only can skills for replacing the alternator in a car or fixing a leaking faucet be acquired through imitation, but lay volunteers can also learn skills for leadership in the parish. The process of imitation typically progresses in this fashion, called the replication cycle:

1. The veteran leader models leadership and the apprentice observes how it is done. In this case, the mentor essentially says, "I'll do it, and you watch me." This is the direction stage.

2. The mentor and the learner undertake the leadership task together, interacting on the project. The mentor invites, "Let's do it together." This is the collaboration stage.
3. The assumptive leader does the primary work of leadership while the veteran leader supervises and intervenes occasionally to correct or redirect the apprentice. Here the mentor counsels, "Now you do it, and I'll watch you." This is the supervision stage.
4. The new leader undertakes to lead the project with newfound confidence, reporting the results of his efforts to his predecessor. At this point, the mentor says, "Contact me if you need me." This is delegation.

The dynamic of imitation is so important in the process of forming new lay leaders that it would be wise to regularize it in the congregation's organizational structure. This happens when a church intentionally links emerging leaders to seasoned leaders in an apprenticeship relationship. Over time, new leaders learn the ropes of leadership before being entrusted with its reins. The veterans embody leadership that can eventually be replicated by their partners.

IMITATION APPLIED TO ORGANIZATIONAL MODELS

Imitation is a dynamic that is vital to forming leaders in a Christian congregation, no matter what its organizational structure is. You can exercise this dynamic in each of the three major models of church organization.

Working Board Application

In the working board model, imitation builds upon the impact of immersion. Recall that in the previous discussion on immersion, the ministry ladder method was commended. In this approach, the volunteers in the church's programs climb the ladder of experience to higher levels of leadership.

An example was provided of Sally, who progressed from Sunday School aide to teacher to superintendent and then on to director of the board of Christian education. She grew in competence in each of these roles not only by being immersed in their activities but also by observing the behavior of her predecessors in these positions and imitating them. As a Sunday School aide, Sally watched the teacher she assisted and thus acquired many pedagogical skills. As a Sunday School teacher, she observed the administrative actions of the superintendent, and in fact, duplicated his approach when she assumed that role. This superintendent role placed her on the board of Christian education, causing her to learn the culture, values, and responsibilities of that board. During her initial two-year term, Sally watched her board director lead the board. This capable lay leader became for her a model for leadership, and so when she succeeded him as director, she had a model to emulate.

Some working board structures employ a formal and intentional process of mentorship. This happens when an assistant director is appointed from the members of the board to become the director's successor. In this case, the congregation expects that the assistant director will become the next director. Accordingly, the current director sees to it that the assistant is primed for leadership by using the replication (direction-collaboration-supervision-delegation) process described earlier. A mentor-learner relationship is purposefully cultivated.

Managing Board Application

Congregational structures that employ the managing model can utilize a similar process. Frequently in this approach, an assistant manager is elected to aid the ministry program director. The purpose of this collaboration is not only to ease the workload of the director but especially to facilitate the training of her successor. In this apprenticeship, the assistant observes the administrative work of the leader and imitates that role in a limited manner.

This apprentice arrangement should intentionally apply the replication cycle. The initial stage of this cycle is direction. The lead manager initially does the work of management and invites the assistant to watch. The assistant attends some meetings of the council of managers (i.e., the gathering of ministry program directors) to witness the council workings. Accordingly, the learner is directed to how the board operates and how the managing role functions. For example, a manager in charge of the youth ministry area demonstrates to the assistant how she identifies, recruits, and trains volunteers to coordinate a youth service event.

The second stage is collaboration. Here the assistant works alongside the lead manager, and both are involved in management. The leader shows how a task is done and then invites the apprentice to give it a shot. In this stage, the work is mutually shared. For example, the youth ministry director asks the assistant to offer a name of a potential lay worker, participate in contacting that worker, and collaborate in the training session for the youth service event.

The third stage of this process is supervision. Here the assistant does the primary work of leadership while the lead manager supervises, all the while providing counsel and correction as needed. The assistant essentially does the task and the director watches and gives commentary along the way. Under the youth ministry scenario, the supervisor gives the assistant an assignment to select, recruit, and equip for service another adult worker who will lead a youth project, all the while the mentor is present to witness and assess the assistant's performance.

In the final stage, delegation, the lead manager releases the apprentice to accomplish a designated outcome for the program area. The manager does not accompany the assistant in this assignment, nor does he directly supervise it. The apprentice is given a deadline, at which time she reports the results of her efforts to the director. In this stage, the assistant in youth ministry might be given an assignment to recruit and train an adult to coordinate communication among the teenagers of the congregation. The assistant is given the ends and limitations of this assignment in a written brief, and a deadline for execution of the assignment is agreed upon. After that date, the assistant delivers a report to the youth program manager, who assesses the effort and discusses with the apprentice what she has learned.

Governing Board Application

It was stated earlier that the governing model poses challenges to the immersion dynamic. The same can be said regarding the imitation dynamic. Since there is no ministry ladder or apprenticeship process in most governing boards, the imitation dynamic becomes more intuitive than intentional. Nevertheless, it is possible for board members in policy-based governance to benefit from imitation.

The imitation dynamic can be applied in the governing board model when a distinction is made between senior members and junior members. Recall that during the first six months or so in this arrangement, the junior members simply observe the processes of policy-based governance. This fulfills the stage of direction in which the senior members in essence say, "We'll do the governance, and you watch us." After this observation phase, the junior members are invited to begin collaborating with the senior members in discerning and articulating ends and limitations policies for the congregation. Next, the senior members ask the newer members to take the lead for certain assignments in which policies and strategies need to be established, all the while giving counsel and aid to their efforts. Here, the senior members say to the juniors, "You attend to this policy need, and we will assist you." Finally, these relative newcomers to the board may be designated as senior members, usually after the first half year in service to the board.

SUMMARY

The organizational structure of a Christian congregation requires lay participation and lay leadership. Churches are to form and equip leaders. This is God's intention for every congregation, for His purpose is "to equip the saints for the work of ministry" (Ephesians 4:12).

Critical to the task of engaging lay board members in the work of the congregation is the development of lay leaders. The congregation raises up these leaders through a process of formation. They are equipped through an intentional process that integrates the dynamics of instruction, immersion, and imitation. When thoughtfully and appropriately applied, this process produces lay leaders who are competent to accomplish the tasks assigned to them.

This process is a recursive one rather than a purely linear one, and it no doubt will be marked by struggles and setbacks. Yet as God's Word is applied, the Spirit of God is at work to raise up lay leaders who experience growth in faith through leadership in the parish. They competently carry out the responsibilities assigned to them and produce fruit for the kingdom of God, advancing His mission in their contexts. This in turn will bring fruitful growth to the entire congregation so it can be faithful to the calling that God has entrusted to it.

This *equipping* process—of instruction, immersion, and imitation—is beneficial to the organizational life of a Christian congregation. It produces competent board leaders. But there is even a higher level that can be attained in leadership formation. That is when leaders are *empowered* for innovation. This is the opportunity that is outlined in the next chapter.

CHAPTER 9

EMPOWERING INNOVATIVE BOARD LEADERS

In the previous chapter, we became familiar with a process to equip leaders for service in congregational boards. The word *equip* is appropriate, for this process provides board participants with the needed knowledge and skills to administer their board responsibilities; they are *equipped* for the tasks assigned to them. The processes of instruction, immersion, and imitation prepare them to carry out the leadership responsibilities with which they have been entrusted by the congregation.

Churches that are served by competent leaders are truly blessed. God is at work through the capable efforts of these saints. Achieving this level of competence in leadership is a wonderful experience for board members. Not all board leaders arrive at this level of competence.

As good as this is, however, it is not the optimum level of functioning that is possible. There remains the potential for even greater effectiveness and productivity. This is achieved when board members are *empowered for innovation*.[95] This happens when lay leaders realize their highest potential for productivity. Not only are goals reached, but they also exceed expectations! This is a time in which board members affirm that God is doing "far more abundantly than all that we ask or think, according to the power at work within us" (Ephesians 3:20).

95 The dynamic of innovation is added to those of information and imitation in Mike Breen, *Multiplying Missional Leaders*, 84–85.

This is all to the praise of God—"to Him be glory in the church and in Christ Jesus throughout all generations" (Ephesians 3:21).

A significant characteristic of congregational leaders at this apex level is that they are highly responsive to the opportunities and challenges of ministry. They recognize opportunities to advance God's mission, and they act upon them. They also quickly perceive obstacles that hinder the strategic advance of the congregation, and they maneuver to address them effectively and positively. Under such innovative leadership, the church board is responsive to changes in its contexts, adjusting as needed. The team develops a prescient ability to anticipate opportunities to advance God's mission.

EMPOWERMENT

Many corporations and businesses have embraced a commitment to empowering their leaders and managers to achieve higher productivity. The word *empower* means "to give power or authority," and it involves releasing leaders to move beyond the maintenance mode and to improve service and performance. This approach has been especially promoted by an influential writer in leadership theory, Ken Blanchard, and his associates. Empowerment involves three keys: (1) entrusting managers with information and authority, (2) releasing them within clear boundaries to exercise autonomy and responsibility, and (3) encouraging them to collaborate with others in nonhierarchical teams.[96]

This approach can be applied in church contexts to empower lay leaders. In accord with the first key, board members are given thorough information for their tasks, as well as insights from the immersion experience and the model of mentors. But then they are trusted to use that information and insights to explore new ventures of ministry.

According to the second empowerment key, congregational leaders are authorized—that is, entrusted with authority—to pursue the accomplishment of the board's purposes and goals with creativity and experimentation. The parish encourages them to take the initiative in

96 Ken Blanchard, with John Carlos and Alan Randolph, *Empowerment Takes More Than a Minute*, Second ed. (San Francisco: Berrett-Koehler Publishers, 2001); Ken Blanchard, *Three Keys to Empowerment*, (San Francisco: Berrett-Koehler Publishers, 2001).

making decisions to solve problems and improve outcomes. This enables them to take the ministry they oversee to a higher level of fruitfulness, all within clearly defined theological, ethical, and fiduciary boundaries.

By appropriating the third key to empowerment—collaborating with others in nonhierarchical teams—congregational leaders invite others to join their cause and gather them into self-directed teams. These teams take on a task and then plan, execute, manage, and evaluate the effort from start to finish. Many of the practices that were commended in the chapter on action teams are applicable to this aspect of empowerment.

For empowerment to flourish, the ground needs to be cultivated. Most importantly, the congregational culture must nurture trust. Veteran leaders who have overseen the formation process of instruction, immersion, and imitation must now release their protégés to lead the boards or ministries. The former leaders give the new board members freedom and power to explore new ways of advancing God's mission. They are trusted and authorized for leadership. This can only thrive in the context of trust.

When this culture of trust is cultivated among church board leaders, the soil is enriched and becomes fertile ground for innovation. And beneficial innovation is at the apex of effective leadership. Leaders are equipped by instruction, immersion, and imitation. But they are empowered for innovation.

INNOVATION

Empowered lay leaders will innovate. The goal here is that the learner not only replicates his mentor's leadership but also goes beyond this to form his own leadership style and to produce his own unique fruit. He explores new opportunities to advance the mission of God in his specific program area. He pioneers new frontiers for executing ministry in the local congregation.

Ultimately, the desired outcome of leadership formation is not merely to clone veteran leaders but to generate creative innovators. God has made each of us to be unique; that results in diversity in the Body of Christ (Romans 12:3–8; 1 Corinthians 12:4–30; 1 Peter 4:10–11). Accordingly, a healthy congregation is guided by leaders whose distinctive personalities, perspectives, gifts, and approaches to ministry will produce a diversity of creative contributions.

The process of leadership formation described in the previous chapter culminated in a new leader imitating his mentor. Imitation is a worthwhile aspiration, but it should not always be the ultimate outcome. Imitation brings the emerging leader to a place of competence. But if he remains at that place, there will be no improvement of the ministry. The status quo may be perpetuated, but progress remains unrealized. As a result, mentors should encourage their apprentices to move forward in the frontier of ministry. Mike Breen describes what this transition from imitation to innovation looks like:

> For a while someone will imitate and copy what you do, but eventually they come to a base level of competency and can start *Innovation*. They innovate through the lens of their personality. They innovate through the lens of their missional context. They innovate as the Holy Spirit shapes them and leads them. The ultimate point is not that a person looks exactly like you. The point is they start there so they can get to the flexibility of innovation.[97]

This flexibility of innovation is what will keep the congregation's ministry fresh and responsive to changing contexts and conditions.

There are good reasons to commend innovation to emerging leaders. One benefit is that innovation makes improvement possible. Imitation brings replication, but innovation brings improvement. The ministry is not only maintained but also advanced. Take, for example, an apprentice who has been prepared to direct the children's ministry of a church. By imitating her predecessor, she will assure that this ministry continues to function adequately. But by innovating, she will lead the ministry to a new level of effectiveness as fresh initiatives are created. What had been achieved by the predecessor is exceeded by the successor. Innovation generates improvement. It has the potential to advance God's mission toward greater fruitfulness.

97 Breen, Mike. *Multiplying Missional Leaders*, 84.

Another beneficial result of innovation is that it allows the congregation to respond appropriately to changing needs and opportunities. We live in a fast-changing society, and the local church should be adept at adapting to changes for the sake of God's mission. This does not mean that the congregation is carried away by every wind of doctrine or is infatuated by every fad. Yet the church should engage cultural changes for the sake of communicating the constantly relevant Gospel. This means that the congregation is responsive to its context. Innovative leaders are adroit at responding to changing needs and emerging opportunities to engage the ever-changing culture with the never-changing Gospel.

The key to facilitating innovation is to release the new leader so that she explores new possibilities and is willing to do some things differently. Leadership scholar Ronald Heifetz advocates for adaptive change in organizations, and he argues that this can only arise from experimentation.[98] This can be a challenge. It is not easy for people, especially those who are new to their responsibilities, to venture beyond the tried and true. It is perhaps even more difficult for long-tenured leaders to approve of and even embrace the changes that are the handiwork of their successors. An example is the director of the youth board who innovates an outreach to neighborhood teens by developing a skateboard park in a previously unused lot that is owned by the church. The veteran leaders may raise eyebrows about the tattooed and gnarly clientele who are attracted to this facility and their integration into the activities of the church youth group. But if the innovation advances the objectives of the youth ministry (ends) and is consistent with the theological, ethical, legal, moral, and fiduciary standards of the congregation (limitations), then the innovator's efforts are within the authority with which she is vested. The pastor, staff, and executive leadership of the congregation should endorse and support the new initiative.

The dynamic of innovation is evident in Timothy's leadership formation process. It is clear that initially Timothy played second fiddle to Paul's leadership in planting churches in Asia Minor and

98 Ronald A. Heifetz, "Leadership, Adaptability, Thriving," *Faith & Leadership*, November 18, 2009, www.youtube.com/watch?v=CSZIdiVlYxc.

Greece. But Paul also trusted Timothy to take the reins of congregations while the apostle went elsewhere. For example, Timothy was left to lead the recently planted churches at Thessalonica, Berea, and Corinth (Acts 17:10, 14; 1 Corinthians 4:17; 16:10–11). Ultimately, Timothy is assigned to be the overseer at Ephesus, a major center of the Christian movement (1 Timothy 1:3). In each of these cases, Paul released Timothy to exercise leadership in these congregations and so to innovate in accordance with the sound doctrine and practice he had learned from the apostle.

One other thing should be said about releasing new leaders to innovate. This is an act of faith. It is not only a demonstration of people's faith in the emerging leader, which is critical to her progress in leadership. It is also an expression of faith in God. As former leaders entrust their successors to carry on the work of ministry, they also trust God to guide and direct these new leaders. In passing the baton of leadership, both the predecessor and the successor trust that the same Spirit who empowered the ministry in the past will continue to do so in the future. Roland Allen, in his classic guide to missionary formation, affirms that the release of new leaders demonstrates faith in the Holy Spirit's power:

> To do this required great faith; and this faith is the spiritual power in which St. Paul won his victory. He believed in the Holy Ghost, not merely vaguely as a spiritual Power, but as a Person indwelling his converts. He believed therefore in his converts. He could trust them. He did not trust them because he believed in their natural virtue or intellectual sufficiency. If he had believed in that his faith must have been sorely shaken. But he believed in the Holy Ghost in them. He believed that Christ was able and willing to keep that which he had committed to Him. He believed that He would perfect His Church, that He would stablish, strengthen, settle his converts. He believed and acted as if he believed. It is that faith which we need today.[99]

99 Roland Allen, *Missionary Methods: St. Paul's or Ours?* (Grand Rapids, MI: Eerdmanns, 1962), 149.

Imagine how the mission of the Church would have been aborted if the apostle Paul had not released successors such as Timothy to carry on leadership. But Paul trusted that God's Spirit would direct them even as this same Spirit had guided him. This is why the apostle ends each of the two epistles to Timothy by entrusting his protégé to God's grace (1 Tim 6:21; 2 Tim 4:22). We do well to likewise entrust new leaders to the Lord's grace and guidance.

APPLICATION TO ORGANIZATIONAL MODELS

Innovation realizes the potential of leadership in Christian congregations. This is true in the context of each of the major models of organizational structures. How this dynamic is executed varies depending on the model, yet the general approach is consistent.

By definition, innovation involves that which is *new*. The word's etymology is to move into (*in-*) what is new (*novum*). Innovation undertakes a novel approach. It embraces a new idea. It brings forth a new product. Accordingly, congregational leaders achieve innovation by addressing problems, processes, and products in new ways with new results.

INNOVATE BY ADDRESSING PROBLEMS

Leaders influence others to achieve a shared purpose. They guide others on the path to the accomplishment of a mutual mission. But regularly, that road is marked with pitfalls and problems. One way to innovate is to engage those problems in new ways.

A common problem that congregations face is unmet needs. These needs can be material, such as for increased funding or improved facilities. The needs may be programmatic, such as the need for early childhood education. The needs may be relational, such as the need to reconcile estranged parties in the congregation. The needs may be spiritual, such as that of preventing attrition among teenagers. Whatever the needs, enterprising leaders will view these problems as opportunities for improvement. They will seize the opportunity to do something new to meet the need and to overcome the problem.

In the working board model, these problems typically surface in the actual doing of the program board's work. For example, in the board of Christian education, the Vacation Bible School director encounters the problem of recruiting teachers for certain grade levels. The adult education coordinator is challenged to locate curriculum resources for instructors. The small group director discovers the need for better communication between groups. Each of these members of the board of Christian education recognize that current efforts are not meeting the need, so they try alternative approaches and attempt new initiatives. As they do so, they innovate.

In the managing board model, the directors of each program area play primarily a managerial role. They both innovate and help those they manage to innovate. Innovations in management arise from problematic issues in managing: the breakdown in communication, a lack of coordination among workers, struggles in recruitment, failures to produce desired outcomes. The manager will examine the problem to identify what has not worked regarding his management. He will then reflect upon options for solving the problem and try out potential solutions. Sometimes, however, the problem isn't with the manager's style or approach. It is with the people he is managing, those he has recruited to do the work. In this case, the manager's challenge is to help the recruits to identify the problem, own it, and then innovate a solution.

The board of directors in the governing board model will facilitate innovation arising from problems of both small and large scope. It does so on a microscale when it becomes aware of policies that are not accomplished by the professional church staff. In such cases, the directors will discuss with the lead pastor or administrative executive issues related to the failure. Thereafter, the board will either revise the policies (which is an innovation in itself) or will press the staff to find new solutions to the shortfall (that is, direct the staff person to innovate).

The governing board innovates on a macroscale when it identifies new significant and systemic needs that the congregation should address. Frequently, these are strategic in nature. It then formulates ends and limitations policies for that need and delegates these to the church staff to execute. This is innovation when a new initiative results from the board's action. Examples of such initiatives include policies impacting outreach to young adults, visitation of inactive members, and the integration of new musical instrumentation in worship services.

INNOVATE BY ADDRESSING PRODUCTS

The goal of church organizational structures is to facilitate the production of good fruit, spiritually speaking. The goal of boards is that the church be productive! Consequently, congregational boards should strive toward improving the products of their efforts. The focus of this innovation is on new and better results.

Smartphones are an important technological product in our society. But these products are continually being improved from one product generation to the next (e.g., the thirteenth generation iPhone is an improvement over the twelfth generation). Tech companies like Apple or Samsung are continually exploring how to improve their products. Innovation often focuses on the product.

In the working and managing board models, innovation happens when the board members take time to plan. Fundamental to planning is the task of setting goals and identifying outcomes. Board members should articulate their intended outcomes clearly and concretely. But they also do well to reflect upon how these outcomes, these products, can be improved. For example, the manager of the spiritual care program already does a good job of seeing that homebound members are visited monthly. But the goal of monthly visitation is improved by integrating intercessory prayer into each visit. The outcome of monthly visitation is enhanced by ensuring that each member who is visited is cared for by prayer.

In policy-based governance, board members innovate products by improving ends policies. The ends policies are in fact the articulation of outcomes for advancing the congregation's purposes and goals. The product is expressed as an end. One of the most important responsibilities of the board of directors in this model is to carefully craft relevant, significant, impactful ends policies. These board members will innovate best when they carefully and creatively craft new ends policies that will result in improvements to the congregation's mission and ministry.

INNOVATE BY ADDRESSING PROCESSES

Sometimes innovation is catalyzed not by a pressing problem, nor by the need for a new product, but because of an opportunity to accomplish the goal in a new *way*. This happens when a board accomplishes its outcomes, but in doing so the leader recognizes a better way to get there. In such a case, what is innovated is not the outcome but the method or means for producing that outcome. The new *process* is the innovation.

The opportunity to innovate processes arises in the working board model because board members, who are doing the work, are directly involved in the processes. They are active participants in the processes—the methods, models, and means—that achieve their assigned goals. It is in their direct participation that workers innovate new and better ways to train ushers (worship board), encourage hospitality (fellowship board), feed the homeless (service board), or promote personal witness of faith (evangelism board).

In the managing board model, the innovation of processes arises as the directors (and their assistants) receive feedback from those they manage. For example, the manager of the children's ministry receives a recommendation from the VBS director to utilize more dramas using actors to better communicate the Bible stories that are being taught. The manager, collaborating with the VBS director, then creates a process for ensuring that such dramatization is integrated into next year's VBS program. This improvement in the means to engage children in biblical narratives becomes an innovation in the VBS ministry.

In the governing board model, as mentioned earlier, the desired product is identified in the ends policies. Frequently the board will be informed that these ends have been achieved by the staff. But the board will also receive a report about the execution of the limitations policies. These policies deal with resources, methods, and practices. In short, they deal with the processes. The report from the staff on the limitations policies will provide fertile insights for changing the procedures in an innovative way. The staff report may actually make recommendations for revising the limitations policies, and oftentimes these are insightful and beneficial.

To improve a limitation policy is in fact an innovation, even though the outcome (end) doesn't necessarily change. For example, the board may receive a report from the staff person in charge of missions that the goal (ends policy) of three foreign mission trips was accomplished. But as a result of the experience of participants in these mission trips, this staff person recommends an additional limitations policy—namely, that candidates be required to pass an inventory on cross-cultural awareness before being approved to participate in the trip. The board assesses the pros and cons of this proposal and then approves a new policy with this requirement. An innovation in the process of approving mission trip participants is the result.

SUMMARY

The organizational structure of a Christian congregation requires lay participation and lay leadership. Leaders are equipped to be competent and empowered to be innovative. God's kingdom is forward moving, and this innovation advances the forward momentum of the kingdom.

Empowering leaders releases them to innovate in ministry and mission. Innovation can result in improvement in accomplishing the Church's ministry and mission, advancing it to a higher level of fruitfulness. Innovation can also promote healthy responsiveness to the changing opportunities and challenges that churches encounter. Releasing leaders to innovate is not only an act of trust in those saints but also a demonstration of faith in the Holy Spirit's work through them.

Leaders innovate by addressing problems with new solutions. They innovate by delivering new and improved products as the outcome of the congregation's efforts. They innovate by developing new processes for advancing the purposes that God has given to His Church. Empowering leaders to innovate is critical to creative ministries that generate from the creative work of the Spirit of God.

CHAPTER 10

INTEGRATING **SPIRITUAL PRACTICES** INTO BOARD **BUSINESS**

Part 3 of this book has identified ways to improve the functioning of the organizational models described in Part 2 by using action teams, equipping practices, and an empowerment approach for board leaders. In this chapter, it is time to return to the focus of Part 1, specifically the *theological* framework for organizing Christian congregations. There we learned that the Church operates in two dimensions, with both a sociological manifestation and a spiritual reality. The presentations on organizational structures, teamwork, and leadership formation in Parts 2 and 3 engaged primarily the sociological dimension (although always performed for the sake of the spiritual priorities—Christ's mission and ministry). Now we will return to a more focused look at the spiritual orientation of Church life. We will attend to ways to integrate spiritual disciplines and practices into the administration of boards, councils, and teams. This is vital to the spiritual wellbeing of churches and their leaders.

Too frequently, church officers and board members find their experience of leadership in congregations to be spiritually dry and draining. Charles Olsen interviewed the leaders of churches from varying denominations and discovered that many experienced spiritual indispositions during their terms of service. He reports:

> "I heard a high level of frustration and even disillusionment among laypeople with their experience on church boards, much of it due to lack of a 'missing' element—spirituality. New members expected that a church-board term would provide an opportunity to develop and deepen their faith. Too often they encountered 'business as usual.'"[100]

Frequently, lay church officers do not grow in faith and spiritual maturity during their time of leadership. Due to the experience of conflict or a lack of productivity, some become jaded in their commitment to the Lord. Once their term is over, they are over with the church. Some even fail to remain engaged in the life of the congregation, including its worship life. Furthermore, spiritual malaise among the leadership can impact and infect the entire membership. This is a sad phenomenon and certainly not God's will.

It is important to remember that the Church dwells in two dimensions, the spiritual and the sociological. When one dimension is neglected, the health and potential of the congregation is affected negatively. This is especially true if the spiritual dimension is neglected because, as we saw in chapter 2, this is the most vital one. Church consultant Mike Bonem asserts that a congregation with an overreliance on secular practices may simply function as a nonprofit corporation rather than as a Christian church and thus relinquishes the transforming power of God.[101]

Rather than neglect the spiritual dimension, we must cultivate it. We cultivate it in all aspects of congregational life, whether that be worship, education, caregiving, or outreach. But we also cultivate it in the administrative arena. The key is to *integrate* spiritual priorities and practices into the organizational activities of boards, councils, and teams. There are ways to bring spiritual vitality to congregational officers, board members, and lay leaders through their experience of leading the church. Some methods can orient participants to grow in faith and discipleship during their terms of service.

---

100 Charles M. Olsen, *Transforming Church Boards into Communities of Spiritual Leaders* (Herndon, MD: The Alban Institute, 1995), xi.

101 Mike Bonem, *In Pursuit of Great AND Godly Leadership: Tapping the Wisdom of the World for the Kingdom of God* (San Francisco: Jossey Bass, 2012), xiv.

What follows is a guide to integrating spiritual practices into the work of lay leaders in churches. These practices may be enacted at the board table or at meetings of the council. They may be used during occasional retreat events or in the routine activities of the board. Leaders may even apply these practices to other contexts and callings.

The spiritual practices heretofore commended are categorized by viewing the description of the Spirit-led congregation provided in Acts 2:42: "They devoted themselves to the apostles' teaching and the fellowship, to the breaking of bread and the prayers." This passage depicts the activities of the first Christian congregation in Jerusalem following the day of Pentecost. On that day, God the Holy Spirit was poured out to indwell those who repented of their sin, believed in the risen Christ, and were baptized in His name (Acts 2:37–41). The *spiritual* dimension is evidenced in how the *Spirit* works in the lives of these new believers. Accordingly, the spiritual practices promoted in the following pages align with what these early Christians devoted themselves to. The first practice is that of *learning*—the apostles' teaching. The second practice is that of *sharing*—fellowship. And the final practice is *praying*—the prayers.

DEVOTING TIME

Acts 2 states that the early disciples devoted themselves to these spiritual practices. That means that they devoted *time* to those activities. Similarly, congregational leaders are to devote time to them. Certainly, they will do so outside the gatherings of their boards, in their personal devotion time, and in their corporate engagement in worship and Bible study. But their experience of administration in the church will be much more spiritually rich and rewarding if they devote some time in their meetings to these practices as well.

If these spiritual practices are engaged in at the council meeting or in the board room, they will consume some meeting time. But if they are made a priority, time can be allotted. I recommend that fifteen to thirty minutes be devoted to these practices on the agenda of a typical board meeting. Some leaders may be able to schedule more time than this. This will mean, however, that the chairman and board members need to be disciplined to use the meeting time wisely.

It is not necessary that all three practices—learning, sharing, and praying—be included in every gathering. They can be distributed throughout a series of meetings. At a given meeting, one might attend to only one or two of the practices. At the next meeting, the remaining practice would be engaged.

Although the activity of learning, sharing, or praying will oftentimes occur at the beginning of the meeting, this need not always be the case.[102] For example, petitionary prayer may be scheduled when major decisions are to be made throughout the course of the meeting. Sharing stories of ministry impact could be distributed at various places in the agenda. Furthermore, although it is helpful to schedule these activities as items on the meeting agenda, some flexibility will be appropriate. The chairman of the meeting should be open to a spontaneous prayer, reflection on Scripture, or sharing of an experience, as the opportunity arises.

Other activities on the meeting agenda can be streamlined to make time for the spiritual practices. For example, the chairman can require that all reports by board members be made in writing rather than presented orally at the meeting. These written reports are distributed beforehand to members of the board by electronic means (email, social networking, etc.) and members are expected to read them before the meeting. Then during the meeting, members may ask questions about items in the reports and receive answers on those questions rather than having members rehearse full reports orally.

Another time-saving practice is to utilize a consent agenda. This packages routine business into one agenda item that is approved in one action (rather than discussing each item separately). These practices save a lot of time in the meeting that otherwise would be spent on oral reports and routine business. You may access other time-saving approaches by searching the Internet on how to make meetings more time efficient.

---

102 Charles Olsen asserts: "Boards need to liberate the Bible from its imprisonment in the 'opening devotions' of the meeting. Those devotions, wedded with an opening prayer, form one of the bookends that routinely hold committee reports together. (Besides, to be a bit cynical, it provides a time cushion for some to arrive late, just in time for the 'real meeting' to begin.) The Bible and a hymnal may be used at any point in the agenda, especially when stories are told." *Transforming Church Boards,* 69.

With these understandings in place, we will now consider the three spiritual practices—learning, sharing, and praying—that may be integrated into board meetings to advance the spiritual health of the participants. I will provide examples of how these practices may be implemented in administrative gatherings. These options are suggestive but in no way exhaustive. I pray that they might prime your imagination to discover practices that fit your context and advance your board's purposes, along with the benefit of bringing spiritual vitality to the participants.

THE SPIRITUAL PRACTICE OF LEARNING

The first practice to be inculcated among congregational lay leaders is that of learning. Recall that in the process of equipping new workers for leadership positions, the task of instruction plays a formative role. Lay officers are informed about their responsibilities early on. They may learn biblical and doctrinal truth as well as leadership theory and methods that are relevant to their roles. They are instructed about the ends to which they are accountable as well as the limitations that bind their authority. This instruction is critical to equip new officers for leadership in the church.

But the spiritual practice of learning extends beyond this preliminary instruction. It should be an ongoing process resulting in continued faith formation throughout a board member's term of service.

The believers who were devoting themselves to the apostles' teaching in Acts 2:42 were just getting started in the Christian life. Yet the verb form employed (*proskarterountes,* present participle) indicates that their devotion to instruction was an ongoing process. Leaders, young and old, continued to receive instruction in the truth of the Spirit from able teachers. The same is true today. All Christians, but especially those who lead, are to be nurtured by instruction in the Word of the Lord.

One cannot overstate the importance of biblical instruction for the wellbeing of a church and particularly of its leaders. Greg Hawkins and Cally Parkinson conducted extensive research to identify the leading factors for spiritual growth and maturity among Christians. They surveyed 157,000 individuals from more than 500 churches and discovered that the most significant factor in promoting spiritual growth is the practice of reflecting on Scripture.[103]

Leaders of a Christian church especially need the spiritual discipline of learning from Scripture. Certainly, pastors and professional staff are to be firmly grounded in the Word of God. But lay leaders also require continued nurture in the Word, both for their sake and for the sake of those they lead. Ted Kober reinforces this reality in his consultation with church leaders. Kober is a seasoned counselor in reconciliation ministry, assisting congregations in conflict. This is what he has observed about the relationship between leaders formed in God's Word and the health of the congregation:

> There are many authors who postulate about what makes a church healthy. However, working for more than two decades with church conflict and reconciliation, I have encountered an underlying cause affecting church health that is not recognized by most writers on this topic as foundational. I observed that the health of a congregation is directly related to how richly the Word of Christ abides in her people, especially her leaders. . . . When the Word of Christ dwells richly within a church's members, they respond to conflict in healthy ways that reflect that indwelling. They respect one another in the midst of disagreement. They reference the Bible when making key decisions. When disputes become heated, they reconcile with one another through confession and forgiveness. They demonstrate spiritual maturity and congregational health.[104]

In order to test this conclusion, Kober set out to interview pastors and lay leaders in eleven churches that were recognized by others to be healthy. He discovered that what these churches shared was not a leadership approach, style of worship, or even organizational structure

103 Greg Hawkins and Cally Parkinson, *Follow Me: What's Next for You?* (Barrington, IL: Willow Creek Resources, 2008), 114.

104 Ted Kober, *Built on the Rock: The Healthy Congregation* (St. Louis: Concordia Publishing House, 2017), 34–35.

and governance. The primary commonality was a high level of participation in Bible study by the members and especially the lay leaders.[105]

It is important that lay leaders be learners of God's Word by participating in the study offerings of the congregation to which they belong. These can be catechetical courses, Bible studies, and forums that address contemporary issues in the light of Scripture. These are educational opportunities to which all members of the congregation are invited and in which the leaders participate as members of the church. In the eleven healthy churches that Kober surveyed, the proportion of lay leaders who participated in Bible study averaged 75 percent.[106] When this happens, the leaders not only grow in faith personally but also model devotion to God's Word. It is not unrealistic or legalistic to expect congregational leaders to participate regularly in at least one ongoing Bible study or instructional course offered by the church during their term of service.

But it is also possible—indeed, highly desirable—that learning in God's Word be a spiritual practice that is engaged in at the council meeting or in the board room. Board leaders should make nurture in the Word a priority for the participants. Sometimes a pastor or staff member can lead the study and discussion. But ordinarily the chairperson and members of the board should facilitate the learning events. This enables a broader participation in and engagement with the Word of God in these board gatherings. The pastor or staff person can provide recommendations for resources or curricula to guide the lay worker in developing the study.

Practices to Promote Learning: Studying God's Word

There are a variety of approaches to learning in the context of board meetings. Participants should discuss the possible practices and agree on which mode is most appropriate to their situation and needs. Following are descriptions of possible learning methods.

105 Kober, *Built on the Rock*, 41–45.

106 Kober, *Built on the Rock*, 43.

Bible Study. A text from the Bible is assigned to be studied during the meeting. This can be approached in a number of ways.

- The *lectio continua* (continual readings) approach involves reading Scripture sequentially over a period of time. Thus, the reading for this month's meeting begins where last month's session ended. This is oftentimes referred to as a verse-by-verse study. For example, the board of discipleship might choose to work sequentially through the Sermon on the Mount (Matthew 5–7) at its meetings to learn from Jesus the meaning and practice of discipleship.
- The *lectio selecta* (selected readings) method involves using biblical texts that are freely chosen by the leader and participants for their study. Frequently, this means choosing a passage that speaks to the matter at hand for that particular meeting. For example, at one meeting, the board of elders might deal with a policy on church discipline and so study together Matthew 18:15–20. At the next meeting, they address the matter of support for the pastor, and so they discuss 1 Timothy 5:17–21.
- *Lectionary readings* may be employed by lay boards in churches that utilize the lectionary in worship services. This benefits the board members as they reflect upon readings they heard the previous weekend and perhaps on which the pastor preached.
- *Topical studies* are a helpful way for group participants to come to a deeper understanding of biblical teachings on particular subjects. So, for example, the board of outreach could study various New Testament passages that support the mandate of the Great Commission. Catechisms, concordances, and dictionaries of theology are good resources for identifying scriptural passages that address doctrinal topics.
- *Bible stories* provide rich content for spiritual growth. The narratives of Scripture present real-life examples of people who struggled in doing God's work and prevailed by His grace. Board participants receive encouragement and guidance while studying the life expe-

riences of biblical characters. Thus, the board of Christian care might reflect on the stories that describe Jesus' care for the sick and suffering. Many of the parables in the Gospels address personal stewardship, and so these stories would be fertile ground for study by the leaders who manage the stewardship area of a congregation's life.

- *A homework assignment* involves a Bible passage to be read and studied before the meeting. A leader might provide study questions to guide the participants in their personal engagement with the text. When the team assembles for its meeting, the time is spent reflecting on and discussing what each member discovered in her study of that passage. The participants share with one another the insights they gleaned from their private study of the biblical text.
- *Electronic Bible teaching* is a helpful resource, especially for participants who feel ill-equipped to lead a study of Scripture. These are recordings of gifted Bible teachers available on disks or accessed online. Streaming video services provide a plethora of Bible study resources that are immediately accessible for use by church groups.[107]

Study of Spiritual Literature. In this approach to ongoing learning, the participants read and reflect on secondary literature related to the Bible but do not directly study the Bible itself. Here are examples of this kind of study:

- In a *doctrinal study,* the members of the group will read and reflect upon writings that analyze and apply Christian doctrines. These writings might be essays from a Christian magazine or theological journal. They could be blogs about doctrinal matters. The participants could focus on a chapter from a theological book. They may

107 Examples of such video services can be accessed at cphfaithcourses.com, rightnowmedia.org, studygateway.com, and smallgroup.com.

take up study of sections of a textbook in systematic theology or a confessional document such as the Augsburg Confession or the Formula of Concord.

- A *historical study* can bring perspective to the functioning of a board or team. For example, the board of worship conducts an ongoing study of the development of the liturgy over the centuries to better understand the meaning and value of the liturgy's components. The board of elders studies the role of elders throughout Church history from the Early Church to contemporary times. It may be especially useful for officers to read and discuss the historical records of the congregation they serve. We can learn much from those who have gone before us.

- Congregational officers regularly direct the practices of the congregation, and so a study of *best practices in ministry* is often beneficial (practical theology). This is especially the case with leaders in the working and managing board models, but it can also apply to directors in the governing board model. Books, published essays, and online videos that present practices for doing mission and ministry in today's context can be rich sources of insight for these leaders. Participants might approach these like a book club, discussing a chapter at a time at each successive meeting. There are many fine resources available—in print and online—which provide practical guidance in ministry areas such as youth, families, outreach, service, and worship. In the case of policy-based governance, the board of directors might study resources that promote best practices in the legal and fiduciary responsibilities that are the purview of the board.

- Sometimes boards are called upon to address *critical social issues* that arise in contemporary society. Examples would be matters of race relations, economic inequality, health and medicine, social justice, care of the environment, and human sexuality. These provide opportunities for Christians to investigate what God's Word has to say about the issues. The board members could discuss documents written by their denominational scholars on these matters in order to respond to such current events with wisdom and impact.

- Lastly, there is great value in reflecting upon *devotional literature*. Since the concern is for the spiritual wellbeing of the participants, devotional material has potential to nourish and uphold the soul. Teammates may agree to spend several minutes each meeting listening to the devotional material and discussing its meaning for their lives. Both classic and contemporary devotional material can be a treasure trove for spiritual succor.

THE SPIRITUAL PRACTICE OF SHARING

The second practice to be cultivated among congregational lay leaders is that of sharing. Acts 2:42 reports of the Christians in the Jerusalem Church: "They devoted themselves to . . . fellowship." The original Greek word that is here translated "fellowship" is *koinonia*. This derives from the root term *koinos*, meaning *common*, so it has to do with holding in common, a sharing together. The Early Church is described as a people who share together. What is it that they shared? What is it that we as believers can share in today?

First, it is clear that Christians share in God Himself. Previously in Acts 2, the apostle Peter exhorted his hearers to be baptized "in the name of Jesus Christ" and promised that they would "receive the gift of the Holy Spirit" (Acts 2:38). Jesus had commissioned that people be baptized "in the name of the Father and of the Son and of the Holy Spirit" (Matthew 28:19). This expresses union with the triune God (cf. Romans 6:3–5). Accordingly, the apostle John affirms that "our fellowship [*koinonia*] is with the Father and with His Son, Jesus Christ" (1 John 1:3). The apostle Paul declares: "The fellowship [*koinonia*] of the Holy Spirit be with you all" (2 Corinthians 13:14). Those who partake in the Lord's Supper receive "a participation [*koinonia*] in the blood of Christ" and "a participation [*koinonia*] in the body of Christ" (1 Corinthians 10:16). Thus, all those who are baptized are united to God. Those who partake of the Supper of the Lord participate in Christ. We share in union with the triune God. This is the vertical *koinonia* with God that is ours in Christ.

It is likely, however, that the use of *koinonia* in Acts 2:42 refers more specifically to a horizontal sharing between believers—a social fellowship. This is clearly depicted two verses later: "And all who believed were together and had all things in common [*koina*]" (v. 44). This means that the early Christians shared *life* with one another. They shared activities and time together. They shared possessions with one another. Those believers who had plenty shared of their resources with those believers who were in need (v. 45). They worshiped together (v. 46). They shared Table fellowship with one another (v. 46). Their hospitality and sense of community attracted others (v. 47).

When God created the first human being, He declared that it was not good for him to be alone (Genesis 2:18). Indeed, every human desires to be accepted and loved by others. We all have an existential need for belonging and support. God made us to be social creatures and placed us in social communities, primary of which is the family. Frequently in the New Testament, the Church is depicted as a family (Matthew 12:49–50; Romans 12:10–13; Galatians 6:10; Ephesians 2:19; 1 Timothy 3:15; 5:1–12; 1 John 3:1–18). A person who is deprived of family is truly destitute. But in the Church, we have family. We *are* family! The Church is God's ultimate answer to the human need for community. In the Church, we belong to God and we belong to one another. We share life together.

The sharing of life together requires not only receiving but also giving. We participate in community not only to have our needs met but also to attend to the needs of others. This is very clear from the description of the original church in Jerusalem, in which some sacrificed of their own resources to care for others (Acts 2:45). Their social interactions were marked by hospitality and generosity (Acts 2:46). So it is with us today in the family of faith. In *koinonia*, Christians love and serve one another (Romans 13:8–10). They bear one another's burdens (Galatians 6:2). They listen to others' stories and comfort and encourage them (2 Corinthians 1:3–4). They forgive one another even as Christ has forgiven them (Ephesians 4:32; Colossians 3:13). They "rejoice with those who rejoice, weep with those who weep" (Romans 12:15). Accordingly, we in Christ's Church have responsibilities in our life together—responsibilities to love, serve, forgive, and give to others as well as to receive from them.

Church leaders participate in this *koinonia* by being involved in the life of their congregations. But they also have a wonderful opportunity to model Christian community as God designed and desires it to be. The responsibility of board members is not just to take care of business; it is also to take care of God's Church, His family. That means to share life together and love together. Board activities bring devoted servants together and offer an extraordinary opportunity for spiritual growth as "iron sharpens iron" (Proverbs 27:17).

Sometimes participation in congregational leadership can result in social exhaustion and spiritual depletion. But it need not be so. In a study of church boards in which *koinonia* was emphasized and enacted, congregational leaders reported that "the most satisfying aspect of service on boards was working closely and harmoniously together to accomplish meaningful work despite differences, diversity, or conflict."[108] By deepening the sense of community among participants, board activities can be contexts in which leaders are spiritually edified rather than drained; they are bonded rather than burdened.

Practices to Promote Sharing: Telling Stories of God's Work

Because *koinonia* is the sharing of life, and since life is a story, what better way to share life than to share stories? People love to tell stories, especially those that involve themselves. People also love to listen to stories, especially those that involve others they know and care about. Accordingly, one way to cultivate *koinonia* among congregational leaders and board members is to encourage storytelling.

Telling stories is especially appropriate for Christian leaders because they gather around the Gospel, which is itself a story. It is the story of God's restoration of His human creatures through the person and work of Jesus Christ. The entire Bible presents one grand narrative of God's intervention into human history to restore His relationship with sinners. In terms of literary genre, almost half of the biblical material is in narrative form. The story of the life of Jesus given in the Gospels is fundamental to saving faith. God's *koinonia* with us is expressed in an ongoing story of His grace and our response of faith.

In the telling of stories, life is shared and relationships are strengthened. Stories build community. As one shares his experience of life

108 Olsen, *Transforming Church Boards*, xiv.

by telling a story, others can respond with a bond of understanding, empathy, and care.

Furthermore, telling personal stories engages the whole person. The one who tells the story reveals much about his entire being—his values, relationships, priorities, perspectives, and attitudes. Similarly, the one who listens to stories is caught up not only in the logical sequence of events but also in the emotions conveyed and the experiences evoked. Storytelling nurtures empathy.

Stories engage the multiple dimensions of what it means to be human: spiritual, intellectual, emotional, vocational, relational, and physical dimension. This is why telling personal stories is so powerful but also so risky. Therefore, trust must be nurtured among the members of the team. They must be confident that they are in a safe place to share their stories from life. When this trust and confidence is established, deep fellowship develops.

In his book *Transforming Church Boards into Communities of Spiritual Leaders*, Charles Olsen proposes practices for cultivating what he calls "worshipful work" among board members. One of those practices is storytelling. Olsen observes that storytelling was the most popular and readily implemented spiritual practice as reported by his research subjects.[109] Thus, the practice of sharing stories about life and ministry is not only easily adaptable to the agenda of board gatherings but also holds great potential for incorporating the spiritual dimension into the business of the board.

In my own application of this practice with administrative board and council members, I promote the use of *good news stories* into meetings. Since we gather around the Good News story of the Gospel, I encourage lay workers to share stories of how the Gospel is lived out in their lives and in their board work. I have distinguished these stories into three main categories: God's work *to* you, God's work *through* you, and God's work witnessed *by* recipients. I phrase these categories in this way because the one telling the story is thereby compelled to focus on God as well as on himself or others. It reminds the storyteller that God is in his midst and active in his life. Naming God as the main

109 Charles Olsen, *Transforming Church Boards*, xiv, 56.

actor in these accounts helps to more explicitly integrate the spiritual and theological dimension into the practice of storytelling.[110]

> ***Stories of God's work to you.*** In this mode, the participants are invited to share stories of how God is working to transform them. Members narrate accounts of God's renewing grace in their lives. These can be events from the more distant past. But most promising are those stories that depict recent experiences. These stories are very personal, and so all members of the board must covenant to confidentiality. The narrator bears witness to how God is working to challenge, correct, comfort, direct, guide, nurture, or empower them. This can describe experiences at home, in the workplace, or with friends. But it can also be about experiences in their conducting of board responsibilities or in church activities.

> ***Stories of God's work through you.*** This approach has the storyteller describe the impact of an event on others rather than upon herself. Yet the story involves her—that is, the one telling the story was an active participant in the story. Her role was as God's agent to bring His love and grace to others through the ministry overseen by that board. For example, in the meeting of the board of Christian care, a board member would tell the

110 Olsen reports that congregational boards that name God in their storytelling tend to be more spiritually healthy. Charles Olsen, *Transforming Church Boards*, 58.

story of a single mom who expressed renewed hope for her future as a result of participating in the church's support group for divorced people. Thus, it was through the efforts of this board (God's work through you) that someone found hope in Christ.

Stories of God's work witnessed by recipients. This happens when you invite those who have benefited from your board's ministry to speak to the board. They could be individuals or groups. They narrate their experience of the event or program that the board has sponsored. The board members who listen are often very touched by these testimonies. They hear first-hand about the impact of their efforts and how God has blessed others because of their labor. These testimonies need not be done in person at the meeting. One can present a prerecorded video or connect online with the one who shares the account. In this way, the board members hear and see the impact of their ministry and find fulfillment in that impact.

These stories are inspiring to tell and to hear. Board members who share such stories are inspired and strengthened in their faith. As a result, the meetings are life-giving rather than life-draining. We witness and celebrate God's gracious work in our midst, which interjects a powerful spiritual dynamic to board meetings. Members depart from their gatherings being renewed in spirit and excited to serve. Storytelling cultivates *koinonia* among the members of the board.

THE SPIRITUAL PRACTICE OF PRAYING

The final activity in which board members may engage to enhance the spiritual dimension of their leadership experience is that of corporate prayer. Acts 2:42 reports that the Spirit-filled believers of the Jerusalem Church devoted themselves to "the prayers" (*tais proseuchais*). The use of the definite article with this noun suggests that "the prayers" were done corporately—as a group. The context also intimates this. The phrase is not likely referring to private prayers done in isolation. Furthermore, the fact that the noun is plural may indicate multiple orations offered by multiple voices—perhaps formulated prayers. Thus, these prayers were shared in community. They are prayers offered among one another, for one another, and by one another.

This is not the only incident in the Book of Acts that depicts gatherings devoted to prayer. Even before Pentecost, the disciples shared in praying: "All these with one accord were devoting themselves to prayer" (Acts 1:14, cf. v. 24). The powerful spiritual impact of corporate prayer is described in chapter 4: "And when they had prayed, the place in which they were gathered together was shaken, and they were all filled with the Holy Spirit and continued to speak the word of God with boldness" (v. 31). The narrative of Acts depicts prayer as a perpetual practice of the early Christians when they gathered together.

Most relevant to our discussion is how frequently prayer was evoked in Acts when the leaders gathered for business or decision-making. For example, this happened when new workers were selected and commissioned (6:6), when Peter was detained by the authorities (12:5), when Barnabas and Saul were sent on a missionary journey (13:3), and when elders were committed to their responsibilities (14:23). Clearly, the practice of corporate prayer was consigned not only to worship services but also to business meetings and to occasions of discernment and decision-making.

Group prayer is a helpful and healthy spiritual practice for congregational leaders today. Prayer is a powerful way to express dependence upon God and confidence in His promises. Since prayer is an exercise of faith, the board or council that prays is engaging in faith formation and faith demonstration. Praying cultivates spiritual discipline as well as discipleship among teammates.

Prayer is an important practice for spiritual leaders. Oswald Sanders distinguishes between natural leadership and spiritual leadership with this comparison:

NATURAL	SPIRITUAL
Self-confident	Confident in God
Knows men	Also knows God
Makes own decisions	Seeks God's will
Ambitious	Humble
Seeks personal reward	Loves God and others
Independent	Depends on God[111]

It is evident that the practice of prayer cultivates the characteristics in the right column depicting spiritual leadership. Prayer expresses confidence in God as we claim His promises. It displays a relationship with God by those who know Him. Prayer seeks God's guidance to discern His will for decisions. Those who pray are humbling themselves before the One who determines their destinies. Adoration expresses love for the Lord, and intercession evokes love for others. Prayer is an expression of utter dependence on the One who alone determines the future.

Of course, we must remember that our acts of prayer are a response to God's acts to us and for us. We pray in Jesus' name because Jesus has reconciled us to the Father. We come to Him with petitions because He invites us. We confess our sins because He offers forgiveness. We pray boldly because He has given us bold promises. God takes the initiative in His relationship with us, even when it comes to prayer. We respond in faith by conversing with Him.

Congregational leaders are wise to integrate prayer into their gatherings and activities. Olsen recommends that this integration be throughout the entire meeting, not only at the beginning and end. He writes: "If we redefine the activity of the people of God serving on church boards and see it as worshipful work, then prayer no longer can be relegated to a book-end position; it will saturate the agenda and thread its way throughout the meeting. Church boards that are 'doing

111 J. Oswald Sanders, *Spiritual Leadership,* second revision (Chicago: Moody Press, 1994), 29.

board differently' are discovering ways to allow prayer to permeate the whole meeting."[112] By integrating prayer so that it saturates and permeates the meeting, praying will become an integral practice of the board. This will elevate the spiritual climate of the gathering and draw upon the Spirit's power to accomplish the purposes of the board.

It should be recognized, however, that some board members will be more familiar with and fluent in prayer than others. No one should be compelled to pray out loud. Pastors and board leaders may encourage the other participants to speak their orison out loud, but they should not require this. Many people fear public speaking, and vocalized prayer may fit this phobia. Leaders will assure participants that they may express prayers silently if they are uncomfortable doing so audibly. They should be assured that God hears their silent prayers. I have observed that over time, many reticent members of boards will eventually offer spoken petitions after listening to others pray. This is a context for growth in the corporate exercise of faith.

Practices to Promote Praying: Talking to God

Not only will board members gather to discuss business with one another; they should also gather to communicate with God. They do so by engaging in corporate prayer. Here are some practical methods to integrate prayer more thoroughly into board meetings and activities.

> ***Scheduled Prayers.*** Opportunities for praying are deliberately planned and scheduled in the meeting agenda. This can be approached in a number of ways.

- Time for prayer is explicitly identified in the written agenda. This is in addition to the traditional opening and closing prayers. Opportune times are at each action item. Since the action item requires the board members to make a decision on the motion, it is salutary to invoke the Lord's blessing on the decision and ask for His guidance.

112 Charles Olsen, *Transforming Church Boards*, 20.

This is an opportunity to seek for His will to be done. I have observed that when participants "speak to the motion" before God in prayer, they are often much godlier in speaking to the motion before one another in discussion.

- Specific types of prayer may be scheduled at appropriate points in the agenda. For example, the meeting would begin with an invocation, which places the name and character of God upon the meeting. Following the reports, a prayer of thanksgiving is spoken, which acknowledges the Lord for what He has accomplished through the board members since the previous gathering. After personal stories are narrated, members may intercede for those described in the stories. As indicated in the previous paragraph, petitions may be offered when business items are discussed and acted upon. If a problem involving sin or a sinful conflict arises in a meeting, the members do well to pause and confess their role in the sin and hear God's Word of forgiveness. Or they may do as Daniel or Nehemiah did by confessing the failure of their people (congregation) and beseeching the Lord's mercy (Daniel 9:1–19; Nehemiah 1:4–11). Finally, the participants can close the meeting with a doxology, praising God for His faithfulness to them.

Formal Prayers. Another option is to employ prayers that are codified and used more formally in the church. These are written works that bear a more liturgical character. Frequently they are found in the various orders of worship used by one's faith tradition, such as collects, litanies, and responsive prayers. There is a rich tradition of devotional and liturgical material from which these prayers may be accessed. A treasury of resources is available from a variety of eras and cultures. The reference to "the prayers" (*tais proseuchais*) in Acts 2:42 likely involved formal established prayers of both Hebraic and Christian form. Today the board chair can incorporate formal prayers into the agenda as she sees fit in order to direct the participants' focus to God, using the shared language of the Church. Here are some sources for formal prayers:

- *Psalms*. The Psalter has been called both the hymnbook and the prayer book of the Bible. These poetic prayers address many conditions of life and encompass a wide range of emotions. The psalms express lament, praise, thanksgiving, entreaty, and trust before the Lord. They are God's Word to us, but they are words designed to be returned to Him in prayer. A leader can select a psalm to be prayed as it fits the issues addressed in the meeting. The Psalms may be prayed in unison or responsively by verse, half verse, or strophe. Or one member can read the psalm out loud while the others listen and pray its words silently.
- *The Lord's Prayer*. This is the prayer given to us by our Lord Jesus Christ, recorded in the Gospels (Matthew 6:9–13; Luke 11:2–4). It is regularly used in worship services and family devotions. But it can also be employed in board gatherings. I have found it to be especially meaningful to slow down the speaking of the Lord's Prayer when used in meetings. Rather than race through its words, which can be done mindlessly, I pause after each petition and allow the participants to reflect on the words and apply them to the issues at hand. At times, I ask them to vocalize how this petition may be done in our midst. For example, at the meeting of the board of outreach, in praying "Thy kingdom come," one participant articulates the request that the mission effort of the congregation expand Christ's rule of grace in the community. When the petition "forgive us our trespasses" is spoken, another participant confesses the congregational members' reluctance to share the Gospel. The petitions of the Lord's Prayer, though simple, are rich in relevance for the

work of any Christian group. A slow and deliberate approach will enhance the spiritual impact of praying the "Our Father" among board members.

- *The hymnal.* Many people assume that the only place to use the hymnal is in the church sanctuary. But it is a resource rich with prayers that may be shared in the board room as well. Hymnals from liturgically oriented traditions include various orders and litanies that may be prayed by the gathered lay leaders, such as the offices of Matins, Vespers, and Compline. If your faith tradition does not utilize such offices, your hymnal will provide a rich source of written prayers in many of the songs and hymns. These can be spoken or sung. The point is to use them in the practice of corporate prayer as a board or council.

Spontaneous Prayers. Although form has its place in the spiritual practice of prayer, spontaneity is also welcome. Board meetings will seem much fresher and livelier if there are moments of spontaneity. And the use of extemporaneous prayers is one way to facilitate such spiritual refreshment. Here are some possible options for promoting spontaneous praying as lay leaders gather for the business of the congregation.

- *Invitation.* As stated earlier, the leader of a meeting should facilitate prayer that permeates the meeting rather than being relegated only to the beginning and/or conclusion (bookend prayers). To achieve this, he may invite prayers to be offered by participants throughout the time spent together. He himself may offer prayers *ex corde* (from the heart—that is, not scripted) as he sees the need and as the Spirit directs. Or he may pause the business discussion at appropriate times during the meeting and invite other members to speak unscripted supplications to the Lord on the issues or needs being discussed. Another possibility is to begin the meeting with an open invitation that anyone who wishes to interject a prayer during the time of the gathering is encouraged to do so. This sets the attitude that spontaneous prayer is welcome throughout the course of the meeting.

- *Intervention*. There are occasions in which meetings can become tense. Board members disagree with one another and may become angry. Sin is manifest in disharmony, unhealthy conflict, and hurtful words. Or perhaps participants are simply frustrated or at an impasse in making decisions. This is a time for intervention by turning to the Lord in prayer. On such occasions, members can take a time-out for prayer.[113] Just as in an athletic event, a time-out is part of the game rules, so also a spiritually oriented meeting will offer the opportunity for members to call for a pause in business, a time-out, in order to devote time to pray. These prayers may be silent, or spoken, or both. My practice with such time-outs has been to begin with a minute or two of silent prayer and then open it up for those who wish to speak out loud their petitions, confessions, or intercessions. This allows participants to refocus on God, to release the contested matter to Him, and to ask for His grace and guidance in the moment. At such times, I have often observed a powerful working of the Spirit to soften hearts, calm tempers, and turn the tide of dissention toward discernment and unity.

SUMMARY

The Church operates in two dimensions, the spiritual and the sociological. Gatherings in a church—not only in worship services and fellowship events but also in board meetings—must give attention to both dimensions. These administrative groups will oftentimes gravitate toward the business side of the equation while neglecting a spiritual focus. As a result, congregational officers frequently experience a term of service that is soul-depleting rather than spirit-renewing. To avoid this dilemma, healthy churches will integrate spiritual disciplines and practices into the administration of their boards, councils, and teams.

113 Charles Olsen, *Transforming Church Boards*, 22.

This is vital to the spiritual wellbeing of the congregation and its leaders. These spiritual practices are learning, sharing, and praying.

Those who gather for administrative business engage in the *spiritual practice of learning* in order to be nurtured in God's Word. The Spirit bestows His grace through this Word, and leaders grow in faith and wisdom by reflecting on it. When boards gather to conduct the business of the church, participants can integrate the spiritual practice of learning by using various approaches to Bible study. They also grow in the knowledge of the Lord and of His will by reading and reflecting on spiritual literature that presents the perspective of doctrinal, historical, or practical theology.

The *spiritual practice of sharing* is integrated into administrative activities when board members share life together. They experience communion with God and community with one another. Church officers practice sharing by telling stories of God's work among them. They bear witness to how God is working in their personal lives (stories of God's work to you). They narrate how God has used them as His agents of ministry to others (stories of God's work through you). And they hear from those who have benefited from these ministry efforts (stories of God's work witnessed by recipients). Sharing involves giving and receiving as members narrate personal stories and listen to those of others.

Finally, board members integrate spiritual practices into their gatherings by participating in *prayer together.* These prayers permeate their meetings. They keep the focus on God and His will. As they gather in corporate prayer, leaders may deliberately plan prayers in the meeting agenda (scheduled prayers). They may utilize written psalms, orders, and litanies (formal prayers). They may encourage impromptu prayers when needed by invitation or through intervention (spontaneous prayers). The practice of praying directs congregational leaders to depend upon God's Spirit and to discern His will.

Church leaders balance administrative business and spiritual growth by integrating these spiritual practices of learning, sharing, and praying. The result is a more Spirit-filled and Spirit-led ministry and mission.

EPILOGUE

Ryan Clemens completed his second term as congregational president of Mount Zion Church and thus was termed out of the role. As he ended this time of service, he did so with a sense of accomplishment and satisfaction. The organizational machinery of the congregation functioned far more efficiently and productively than when he had begun presiding over the church's leadership four years earlier.

Early in his first term of service, Ryan had expressed frustration about the effectiveness of Mount Zion's organizational design and functioning. He discovered that other officers in the congregation shared his frustration. So together they engaged in prayer that God would guide them to be better stewards of the resources of talent and time offered by members of the congregation. They collaborated to analyze and identify what in the system hindered effectiveness. They also learned about different options for structuring their boards and council. Finally, by researching the best practices of other churches, Ryan and his colleagues were able to gain insight into improving the organizational design and spiritual orientation at Mount Zion.

After considering the findings of this study, the church officers decided against a wholesale restructuring of the congregation's organization. Instead, they opted to refine and improve the existing design. The structure was streamlined to eliminate unnecessary positions on boards. Those who held elected positions were given wider latitude and authorized to act with fewer procedural hoops. These officers felt competent to lead because they had been duly equipped to accomplish the outcomes assigned to them. An ethos of trust was cultivated in the parish that empowered the leaders to venture into innovative approaches of mission and ministry. They experienced spiritual growth as a result of their participation in the administrative functions of the congregation.

Over time, a culture shift developed among the lay leaders of Mount Zion Church. For one thing, more time and energy were invested into action than into meetings. Secondly, participants perceived a movement from bureaucracy to ad-hocracy. Short-term action teams became prevalent in the church. Volunteers were recruited for specific outcomes and organized as teams to accomplish those ends. More members were willing to be involved because of the focused and timely experience of their service. The church's core value of *parishioner participation* was not only realized but was also elevated to achieve a value of *parishioner productivity.*

Above all, Ryan was gratified by the spiritual growth and maturation of discipleship that he observed among the participants. Being nurtured in God's Word, volunteers willingly exercised their Spirit-bestowed giftedness. They were empowered to grow as disciples and stewards in Christ's kingdom. Ryan rejoiced to witness so many sisters and brothers in the congregation who were built up in the Body of Christ.

Ryan reflected on his time of leadership at Mount Zion Church, and he thanked God for the opportunity to serve and to share his talents. He also recognized that he had received much in the experience of leading the congregation, even as he had given much. Indeed, he had grown in his faith and discipleship during these two terms as church president more than at any other time of his life. Ryan bowed his head and thanked the Lord for the opportunity to lead God's people. He embraced the privilege of organizing them for mission and ministry.

God wills that all His baptized children are engaged in service to others. He desires that they be involved in ministry and in the advancement of His mission. Some of that ministry and mission is carried out in the name of the local congregation through its programmatic offerings. Not only do pastors and professional staff participate in this work, but laity should also be participants. Indeed, the clergy's role is to engage and equip laypeople to participate in the mission of God.

Such participation requires organization. And organization requires structure—a design that facilitates efficient, effective, and fruitful labor. Administrative structures are tools for achieving the purposes of the congregation and for advancing the priorities of the Lord.

A Christian congregation is challenged to balance properly the organic nature of the Church with organizational realities. It must integrate both the spiritual and the institutional dimensions. Although churches of all sizes will require some organizational structure, the form of that structure can vary from context to context. The congregation is at liberty to adopt the form of structure that best serves its purposes and God's priorities, within the bounds of God's revealed will in Scripture.

The three dominant models of organizational structures detailed in this book are used by most congregations in North America today. The working board model is so named because those participating on the boards are assigned to do the operational work directly. The managing board model expects those who are elected to manage the work done by others in various ministry areas. The governing board model does the work of governance by providing strategic direction via policies that are then executed by paid staff and lay volunteers. Each of these board models possess potential strengths and weaknesses. The leaders and members of a given congregation must discern which model serves its interests best in the church's distinctive context.

Of course, these organizational structures are not ends unto themselves. They are means to ends. Those ends have been determined by the Lord Himself, specifically to make disciples of all peoples through the faithful use of His Word and Sacraments. These ends have been entrusted to God's Church, which gathers in local congregations. Such churches can benefit from thoughtful, strategic, and sanctified employment of organization for the sake of Christ's mission and ministry.

May you, as a pastor, staff member, or lay leader of a congregation, be guided by the insights of this book to engage the organizational dynamics of your church to the service of God's saints, the advancement of His mission, and the glory of His name!

APPENDIXES

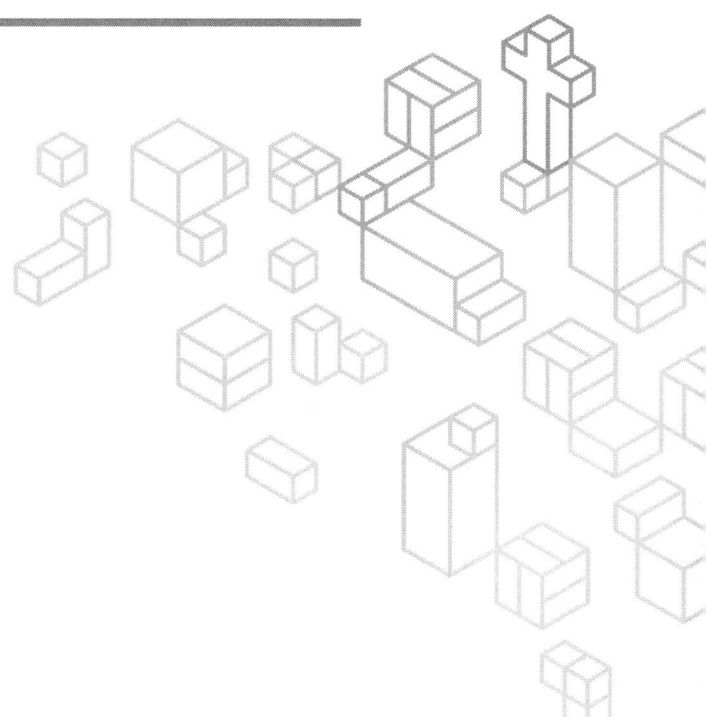

Three documents are beneficial to organizations of all types, whether governments, businesses, clubs, or churches. These documents are a constitution, its bylaws, and an organizational chart. The following two appendices show the usefulness of these resources for Christian congregations and describe how they are developed.

Appendix 1 defines what a congregation's constitution and bylaws are and what they are designed to accomplish. It also explains how to formulate a constitution and bylaws for your congregation.

Appendix 2 explains the purpose and content of an organizational chart and demonstrates its value for congregations. It offers guidance for developing such charts and provides a sample of an organizational chart for a hypothetical ministry.

APPENDIX 1

THE CONGREGATION'S **CONSTITUTION** AND **BYLAWS**

Most Christian congregations in the United States have formal documents that define and direct how the congregation is organized and governed. These documents are called the constitution and bylaws of the church. This appendix will enable you to understand what the constitution and bylaws are and why they are important. It will also guide you in developing or improving them for your own congregation or ministry.

Nowhere in the Bible is a constitution or bylaws mandated for a Christian congregation. These documents are not essential to the theological definition of the Church or to its spiritual dimension. But they are beneficial to how congregations operate in the sociological dimension. Since congregations are composed of people, it is helpful to provide a mutually agreed upon document that defines and guides how the people will work together and be organized. Because a congregation may interact with society and the state, the constitution and bylaws may be required by the secular government for legal incorporation as a not-for-profit organization. For these reasons, it is important to give attention to these documents in your church or ministry.

WHAT IS A CONSTITUTION?

A church's constitution is a document that clearly and concisely articulates the broad principles and structure that govern the affairs of the congregation. It is a formal document that provides direction and organization to the congregation. It broadly articulates the basics: what the congregation is as a human institution, what it is to do, and how it will do so.

The New Testament does not prescribe constitutions for local churches, so there is latitude in designing one. Constitutions will vary from congregation to congregation because each church is unique. Nevertheless, there are some common elements to most church constitutions. Sometimes the denomination or civil government will require certain components to a constitution in order to be accepted. Usually, the constitution of a local church will contain these items:

1. *The Name of the Congregation.* This is identified in order to incorporate as a nonprofit organization in the eyes of the state.
2. *A Statement of Purpose or Mission.* This identifies why the organization exists. For a Christian congregation, this should be guided by what the Bible says is the congregation's purpose.
3. *Confessional Standard.* In this section, the congregation identifies the authoritative standards for what it believes, teaches, and confesses. In the LCMS, this will be the Bible and the Lutheran Confessions.
4. *Denominational Affiliation.* Here the congregation identifies if it is affiliated with a larger church network or denomination. An LCMS congregation will claim its membership in the Synod.
5. *Requirements for Church Membership.* The constitution clearly defines who can be a member of the congregation as well as the rights and responsibilities of membership. It should also articulate how people can be removed from membership (church discipline).

6. *Professional Leadership Positions.* The congregation's constitution will identify key church roles such as those of called workers (e.g., pastor, staff members). It will define how people are placed into those leadership roles as well as how they may be removed from the roles.
7. *Authority.* The constitution identifies the line of human authority for governance and decision-making.
8. *Meetings.* The document will articulate how governance meetings (e.g., voters assemblies and church councils) are called and constituted.
9. *Officers and Boards.* The congregation's constitution will identify the executive lay leadership roles and may list the governing boards of the church.
10. *Amendments.* The constitution should describe the process for making changes in the items above.

These major components of a constitution are regularly called *articles.* Thus, for example, category 5 above would be referred to as the article on church membership.

A church should aspire to two characteristics in its constitution: clarity and brevity. The document's wording should be clear and unambiguous. It should also say only what is absolutely necessary and no more, so that the document doesn't become overwhelmingly lengthy and verbose.

WHAT ARE BYLAWS?

A church's bylaws contain rules that are subordinate to the constitution and provide greater detail and specificity to how the parish will operate. The bylaws spell out many aspects of how a congregation is managed as an organization. They expand and put into action the themes of the constitution, providing directives for the day-to-day business of the congregation. They are a more concrete and contextual set of operational rules than the articles of a constitution. The bylaws are to align with the constitution, and the constitution is enacted by the bylaws.

Because they are highly contextual, bylaws may need to change as the church's context changes. This is why bylaws are more frequently revised and updated than a constitution. They embody the basic ideas of the constitution yet remain fluid enough to be changed to fit the changing needs and conditions of the congregation.

An example of the distinction between a constitution and bylaws is as follows: The constitution would state that the voters assembly must be convened at least once a year for the purpose of approving the annual budget and for electing congregational officers. The bylaws, however, would give more detail, specifying when during the year the voters assembly would meet, how many meetings there would be, how motions and resolutions are submitted and approved, what the quorum for the meeting is, who presides over the meeting, how parliamentary procedure is followed, and so on. The fundamental directive given in the constitution on the voters assembly will not change, but the operational rules that are detailed in the bylaws may change as circumstances change.

Another example of how the bylaws differ from the constitution is evident in the treatment of the congregation's ministry program boards. Ordinarily, the constitution will simply list the prescribed boards—education, evangelism, worship, stewardship, and so forth. It may also provide a brief description of the purpose of each board. The bylaws, however, will provide more detailed information about each board, such as the number of members, the frequency of meetings, its budget, support resources, powers and limitations, and more specific objectives to be pursued by the board.

WHY ARE THE CONSTITUTION AND BYLAWS NEEDED?

There are several practical reasons for a church to have a constitution and bylaws. The constitution and bylaws help a congregation to maintain efficient and orderly activities so that its mission and ministry can be carried out effectively. They provide clarity to the congregation's members about the church's organizational structure and lines of authority. They provide a mutually agreed upon purpose and way of advancing that purpose. They maintain order in the operations of the church and sustain continuity in the way in which the congregation is governed and organized.

As was stated earlier, because a congregation may interact with the state, the constitution and bylaws may be required by the secular government for legal reasons. Without a constitution and bylaws, most Christian congregations will not be allowed by their city or state to be incorporated and be exempt from taxes. The civil government may not even allow the congregation to own property or hire workers without a constitution. Because these are legal documents, the constitution and bylaws protect the church from lawsuits.

The most important thing to remember about the constitution and bylaws is that they are resources to aid in accomplishing the mission and ministry of the parish. These documents are not ends unto themselves but means to the ends. The ends are the advancing of the kingdom of God and the exercising of His Keys to the kingdom. The constitution and bylaws help the members of a congregation organize themselves and administer their resources for the furtherance of these ends.

In summary, a church needs the constitution and bylaws for the following reasons:

- *Unity.* The members of the congregation work together following mutually agreed upon rules and purposes.
- *Witness.* These documents are a testimony both internally to members of the church and externally to the civic community of the priorities and practices of the congregation.
- *Order.* The constitution and bylaws provide an orderly way for congregations to conduct their efforts and activities, preventing chaos in which "everyone does what is right in his own eyes" (Judges 21:25).
- *Clarity.* The documents guide the congregation's leaders and members to operate in ways that are mutually understood, thus reducing confusion.
- *Effectiveness.* The constitution and bylaws promote fruitfulness by following procedures that are tried and proven.
- *Protection.* These are legal documents that protect the congregation from malpractice from within and prosecution from without.

HOW ARE THE CONSTITUTION AND BYLAWS DEVELOPED?

If your congregation does not have a constitution and bylaws, it is probably wise to develop them. Here is some advice for doing so.

First, receive guidance for formulating the documents from the denomination to which the congregation is affiliated. For churches belonging to The Lutheran Church—Missouri Synod, you may download the written resources entitled "LCMS Guidelines for the Constitution and Bylaws of Lutheran Congregations" or "Guidelines for Constitutions and Bylaws of Small and Developing Lutheran Congregations." You can access these by going to the LCMS website (lcms.org) and following this path: Resources → LCMS Document Library → Search Field, where you enter the document title. These documents give you guidance for composing your own congregation's constitutions and bylaws.

Second, find someone who is knowledgeable about church constitutions and bylaws to consult with. This person may be already active in your ministry. Or he may be a member of another church but be willing to assist you. One viable option is to receive guidance from denominational resources. For congregations in the LCMS, leaders should contact the office of their district president and ask for the resources of a district executive to assist them. Many districts of the LCMS have experts who are quite knowledgeable and can guide your congregation through the process of developing these important documents. Most districts have a Constitutional Review Committee that approves constitutions. Typically, members of that committee can provide assistance in drawing up a constitution and bylaws for your congregation.

Third, study the constitutions and bylaws of other congregations and ministries. It is best if these churches are similar to yours. Fortunately, you don't need to write these documents from scratch. You can get good ideas from the examples of others. Nonetheless, be sure to compose your ministry's constitution and bylaws so that they serve the unique needs of your distinctive context.

CONCLUSION

The apostle Paul wrote to the Corinthian Church that "all things should be done decently and in order" (1 Corinthians 14:40). That includes the things related to the organization and administration of your church or ministry. The use of a constitution and bylaws will help the members of your congregation to carry out its work in a more decent and orderly manner. This in turn will promote greater efficiency and effectiveness, all so that the mission of God might be advanced and His kingdom expanded through the faithful use of His Word and Sacraments.

ORGANIZATIONAL **CHARTS**

Local Christian congregations will benefit from using an organizational chart. This diagram, which often is abbreviated as an "org chart," enables all who participate in the organization to visualize the organizational structure of the congregation or some element of its ministry.

WHAT IS AN ORGANIZATIONAL CHART?

An organizational chart is a graphic depiction of the organizational structure of the congregation or ministry. It displays the relationship of the positions or roles in the organization. It is a visual representation of the organization that illustrates the jobs within it and how they relate to one another, including the line of authority. In previous chapters of this book, org charts were provided for each of the three basic models of structures: working, managing, and governing boards. For example, here is the organizational chart for the managing board model:

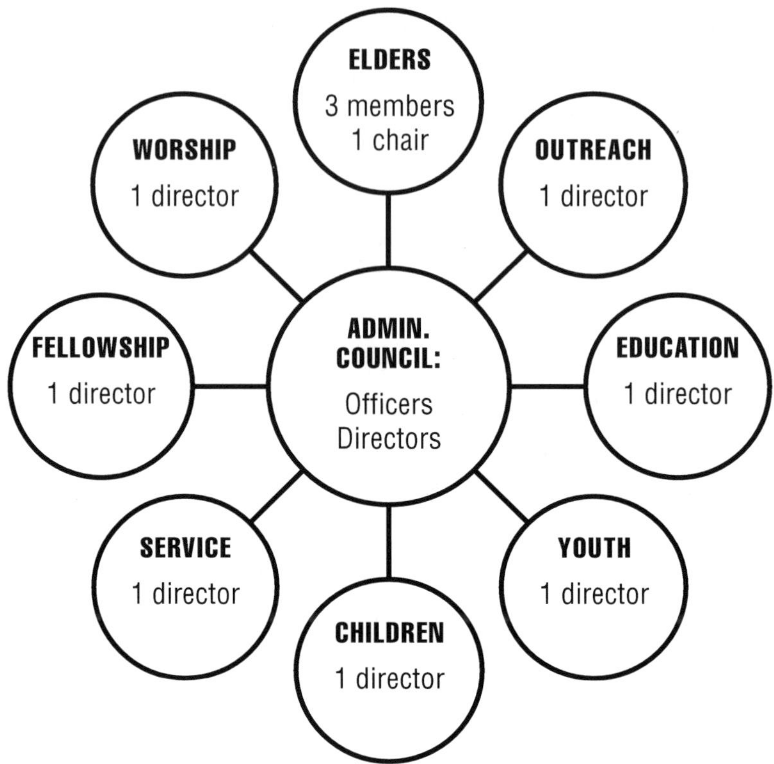

You can see in this graphic display the various program areas of the church (worship, fellowship, service, outreach, education, etc.) and how they connect via the administrative council. It also identifies who is responsible for each element of the organization structure. Each program area has one director, and the administrative council is composed of these program directors as well as the church officers (president, vice president, treasurer, and secretary).

Note how this organizational chart enables you to visualize graphically how the leadership is ordered and how responsibility is distributed to leaders in the congregation. Frequently in an org chart, the progression of authority is displayed hierarchically so that the highest authority is located at the top of the chart and the level of authority decreases as one moves downward in the chart. An example of this approach is shown in the org chart for the governing board model:

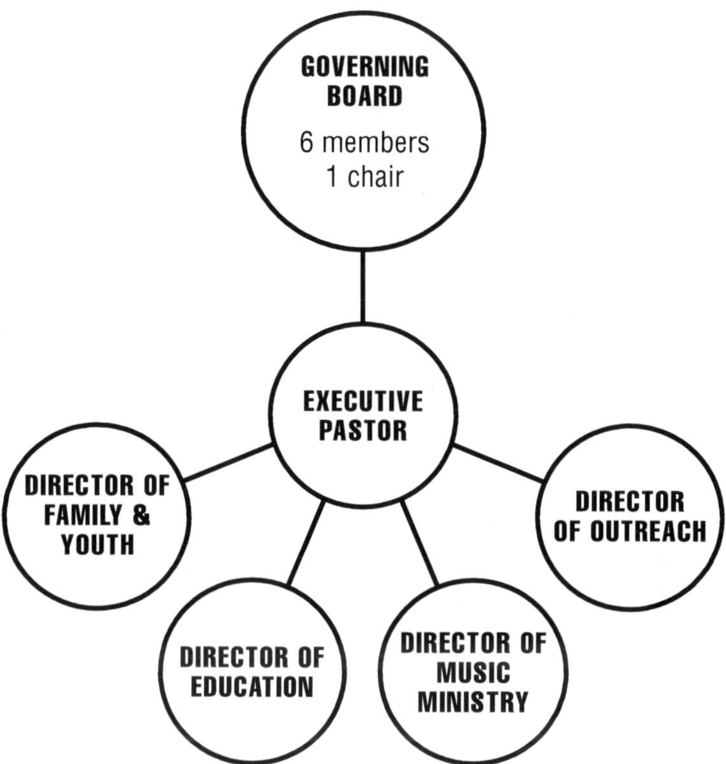

In this illustration, the Board of Directors is the highest authority in the congregational governance, and the Executive Pastor is next in authority, while the program staff (Directors of Family and Youth, Education, Music, Outreach) are subordinate to the pastor. The Board of Directors delegates responsibilities to the Executive Pastor, who then delegates them to the appropriate staff worker to get the tasks accomplished. Once again, the org chart helps you to see how the governance of this congregation is structured.

Consequently, the organizational chart of a church or one of its constituent ministries is a graphic visualization of the structure of the organization showing the relationship of the positions within it and how these are ordered in a line of authority.

WHY IS AN ORGANIZATIONAL CHART NEEDED?

There are several practical reasons for a church to have an organizational chart. The first reason is that *visualization facilitates implementation.* Oftentimes, people can't do something unless they first see it. For example, a construction crew cannot build a new house without the visual blueprints, which lay out the building's design. A football team can't score touchdowns without a playbook, which graphically shows the plays for each teammate to follow. Similarly, an org chart enables participants to visualize how the roles and relationships in the organization are to interact with one another. In a church, this helps both employees and volunteers to understand how the church governance works and to participate in that governance in an effective and productive manner.

A second purpose for an org chart is that it helps the members of a church *to understand the order of responsibility that has been agreed upon and to operate within that order.* The Bible states that in the Church "all things should be done decently and in order" (1 Corinthians 14:40). An org chart helps people to know how to do things in order. The chart clarifies who is responsible for what, who reports to whom, who makes decisions, and who carries them out. It illustrates the chain of command, the lines of authority, and the reporting relationships in the organization. It provides order to the organization.

The third reason to utilize an org chart is because it *enables participants in the organization to relate well with one another.* In other words, it facilitates healthy relationships by

- identifying who are the leaders and who are the followers,
- helping people relate to one another appropriately and productively as they follow the lines of reporting,
- clarifying one's authority and accountability in the institution,
- articulating boundaries for who is responsible for what,
- promoting responsible interaction between participants,

- enabling appropriate delegation of tasks, and
- raising up new leaders in an organization.

In summary, the org chart helps members of the congregation to visualize the congregation's organizational order, to understand their place in it, to operate effectively within that order, and to relate well with others who are in the order.

WHO IS INCLUDED IN AN ORGANIZATIONAL CHART?

The org chart identifies positions and persons in an organization. In a church, the chart should show where each employee fits into the organizational structure. This would include paid staff such as pastors, administrators, teachers, and directors (e.g., director of Christian education, director of outreach, director of worship). Employees who fill either full-time or part-time positions should be included in the chart.

Many churches and ministries depend upon volunteers (who are not employed or paid) to carry on much of the necessary work. It may be appropriate to include the positions of these volunteers in the organizational chart.

The chart should display the positions (role titles). Some org charts will also provide the names of the persons who fill those positions. For example, the following chart displays both the ministry positions and the names of those in the positions:

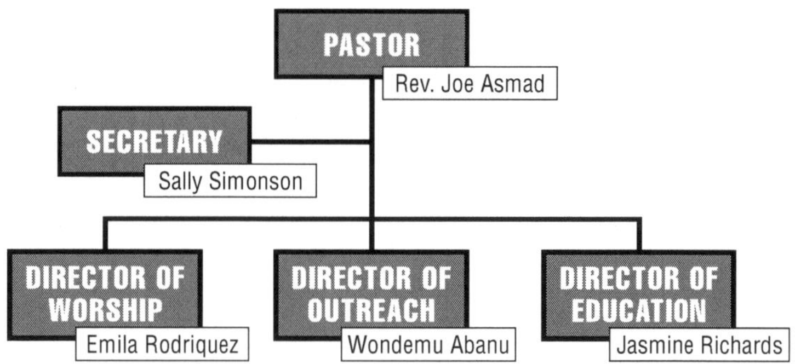

As you can see from this illustration, the primary positions of employees in this church are identified: the pastor, secretary, and directors of worship, outreach, and education. Also, the line of accountability is given—the secretary and the directors report to the pastor. Finally, the names of the people who fill these positions are provided (these would change if the person resigned and is replaced by another employee). It is also possible that the directors of worship, outreach, or education might be unpaid volunteers. So even though they are not paid employees, they are still included in the organizational chart because of the importance of their positions.

HOW IS AN ORGANIZATIONAL CHART DEVELOPED?

An org chart is a visual graphic of the structure of a congregation's governance. It displays the design of the church's organization. It should be arranged according to the following two principles:

1. *Hierarchy of Authority*. The higher the authority in the structure, the higher toward the top of the chart the position is placed. In the example on the previous page, the position of the pastor is at the top of the chart. This indicates that he has the greatest level of authority and oversight in the organization. The positions below on this chart are those roles that are subordinate to the pastor, and the people in those roles are accountable to him.
2. *Categories of Programs*. Each important ministry program in the church, and the person responsible for overseeing that program, is identified. In the example above, there are three program areas—worship, outreach, and education—and the names of the directors of these programs are listed.

With an awareness of these two principles, you can develop an org chart by following this process:

1. Choose a tool for designing the org chart. These are available through several different digital venues. The simplest and most commonly used tools are found in Microsoft Word or Microsoft PowerPoint formats. For more complex charts, you may consider using tools available through Google Sheets. There are other resources with more robust functions available as well, but these involve a fee, such as Lucid Chart (www.lucidchart.com) and Pingboard (www.pingboard.com/org-chart-software).
2. The digital tool will provide options for various templates of organizational structures. You should choose the one that best fits the design of your church's organization. Download this to save as an electronic file that you will be able to work with.
3. Fill in the blocks from top to bottom, according to the hierarchical line of authority in your church or ministry. If your org chart displays employees, the pastor will most likely be at the top of the chart, with staff workers below him. If your chart displays program boards, the governing council will most likely be at the top, with the ministry boards below it. The goal is to display clearly the hierarchy of authority and the categories of programs in the graphic. You should at least identify the titles of the positions in your ministry. If possible, also include the names of the persons who fill each position.
4. Below the visual depiction of the org chart, provide a brief written commentary of the roles and responsibilities of each position and how those positions relate to one another. This will be illustrated in the example provided below.
5. Share your org chart and its commentary with other leaders in your congregation to get their feedback on it. Ask them if it accurately represents the structure of your organization, the line of authority in it, and the relationships of the positions within it. Then revise the chart and its commentary according to the recommendations of these colleagues.
6. Once your proposed org chart is designed, submit it to the governing body of your congregation for its approval. This provides you with authorization to function according to the org chart.

CONCLUSION

A well-designed org chart of your ministry will provide clarity to you and the leaders of your church about how the ministry is organized and how it functions. You will need to update it as people come and go from their positions. You should also revise it as the structure of the church changes to meet the needs of its members and surrounding community. The goal is that all members of your organization understand its structure and operate effectively and efficiently within it, all to the glory of God and the advancement of His kingdom.

SAMPLE ORGANIZATIONAL CHART

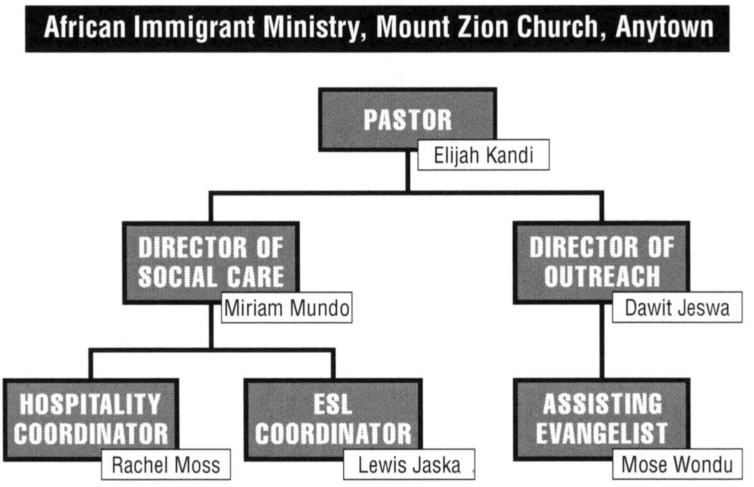

The African Immigrant Ministry of Mount Zion Church seeks to welcome and support both immigrants and refugees from the continent of Africa. God loves each person and desires that each be brought into His community of faith, the Church. God is also bringing many people from Africa and settling them in our city of Anytown. Thus, we seek to reach out and welcome these immigrants and bring the message of God's love in Jesus Christ to them. To do so, we use the organizational structure illustrated above. Here is how the positions (and the persons filling them) interact with one another.

PASTOR (Elijah Kandi): The pastor provides oversight over the African Immigrant Ministry. In the Bible, pastors are referred to as *overseers* (Acts 20:28; 1 Timothy 3:1–2; Titus 1:7), and so it is the responsibility of Pastor Kandi to oversee the doctrine and practice of this immigrant ministry. In addition to his regular functions of preaching, leading worship, teaching, and providing pastoral care, he supervises the directors of social care and outreach, directing and supporting them in their specific responsibilities.

DIRECTOR OF SOCIAL CARE (Miriam Mundo): This position sees to it that the African immigrant members of Mount Zion Church are cared for in their needs of body and soul. The director of social care also works with the director of outreach when he identifies a prospective member who needs social care. Miriam leads the course in "Life Skills for New Americans," in which immigrants are oriented to the culture and civic regulations in the United States, specifically in the local community of Anytown. She also sees that members can find educational resources for their children. She also provides groceries from the food bank to those needing assistance. In these services, she shares the love of Christ and the message of His Gospel. She reports to Pastor Kandi and directly oversees the work of her two assistants, the hospitality coordinator and ESL coordinator. The director of social care is employed for twenty hours per week.

HOSPITALITY COORDINATOR (Rachel Moss): The primary responsibility of this position is to assist African immigrants in finding affordable housing. Rachel works with local government officials as well as the Christian Development Project to locate living accommodations for needy immigrant families, both members of Mount Zion Church and nonmembers. The hospitality coordinator is employed for ten hours per week. This position reports directly to the director of social care and is accountable to that director.

ESL COORDINATOR (Lewis Jaska): This position involves coordinating the ESL (English as Second Language) program at Mount Zion Church. Lewis teaches the sessions but also recruits and equips volunteers to be conversation partners with new immigrants seeking to speak English better. The ESL coordinator is a volunteer position because Lewis offers his services free of charge. Lewis invests ten to fifteen hours a week to this job. This position reports directly to the director of social care and is accountable to that director.

DIRECTOR OF OUTREACH (Dawit Jeswa): In this position, Mr. Jeswa guides the members of Mount Zion Church to bear witness to Jesus Christ in their community. He leads training sessions in evangelistic methods to members of the congregation. He also trains members to make follow-up calls to visitors and potential members. He reaches out to immigrants in the Anytown community to connect needy families with the church's director of social care and to show the love of Christ to those in need. Dawit is employed for twenty hours per week and reports directly to the pastor.

ASSISTING EVANGELIST (Mose Wondu): Mr. Wondu was trained as an evangelist in his home country of Ethiopia. After moving to the United States, he was trained and employed as a computer programmer but still seeks to do evangelism for the church on a volunteer basis. He visits homes and community centers to share the Gospel. He reports directly to the director of outreach but also collaborates with the pastor.